The Indian History of British Columbia
The Impact of the White Man

THE
INDIAN
HISTORY OF
BRITISH
COLUMBIA
THE IMPACT OF THE
WHITE MAN

Wilson Duff

ROYAL **BC** MUSEUM

Victoria, Canada

Published by the Royal BC Museum, 675 Belleville Street, Victoria, British Columbia, V8W 9W2, Canada.

Printed in the United States of America.

See page 184 for the printing history of the book and production information on this edition.

Canadian Cataloguing in Publication Data
Duff, Wilson, 1925-1976.
The Indian history of British Columbia : impact of the white man

Previously published under title: The Indian history of British Columbia, volume 1, the impact of the white man, 1992.
Includes bibliographical references: p.
ISBN 978-0-7718-9483-1

1. Indians of North America – British Columbia – History. 2. Indians of North America – British Columbia – Government relations.
I. Royal British Columbia Museum. II. Title. III. Title: Impact of the white man.

E78.B9D83 1997   971.1'00497   C97-960273-4

Contents

Foreword to the New Edition   8

Foreword to the 1992 Edition   9

Acknowledgements   11

Introduction   13

The Indians of British Columbia   17
The Problem of Indian Names   17
The Classification of Indian Groups   20
   Major Ethnic Divisions   20
   Linguistic Subdivisions   23
   Tribes and Bands   24

Population   53
The Aboriginal Population   53
   Population in 1835   53
   Population Before 1835   54
   Density and Distribution   55
Changes Since 1835   56
   Rapid Decline   58
   First Censuses   61
   Checking the Decline   62
   Rapid Increase   62

The Present Indian Population   64
  Two Kinds of Indians   64
  A Young Population   67
  A Scattered Population   68

The Impact of the White Man   72
The Fur-Trade Period: Stimulus to Growth   73
  First Contacts   74
    First Impressions   77
    The Nature of the Trade   78
  Changes in Native Life   79
    Native Trade   80
    Potlatching   81
    Art   82
    Guns   83
The Colonial Period: Formative Years   84
  Beginnings of Indian Administration   85
Period Since Confederation: Years of Change   87
  Development of Indian Administration   89
    Indian Reserves and Indian Title   91
    Treaty No. 8   98
    Indian Administration Today   100
  More Changes in Indian Life   106
    Material Culture   108
    Arts and Crafts   113
    New Economic Directions   126
    Religious Change: Conversion to Christianity   128
    Social Disorganization   149
    New Forms of Political Organization   154

Appendix 1: Phonemes and Phonetic Key   159

Appendix 2: First Nations of B.C., 1997   164

Bibliography   168

Suggested Reading   175

Index   177

MAPS

1. Indians of B.C.: Major Ethnic Divisions   21
2. Indians of B.C.: Linguistic Subdivisions   23
3. Indians of B.C.: Population Distribution, 1835   57
4. Indians of B.C.: Population Distribution, 1963   69
5. Indian Agencies and Agency Offices, 1963   91
6. First Nations of B.C., 1996   166
7. First Nations Languages of B.C., 1996   167

TABLES

1. Indians of B.C.: Linguistic Subdivisions   22
2. B.C. Indian Tribes and Bands, 1850-1963   27–52
3. B.C. Indian Population, 1835-1963   55
4. Indian Agencies of B.C., 1963   90
5. First Nations Names, 1997   165

Foreword to the New Edition

In the 50 years since Wilson Duff's classic study was first published there have been many changes in the way interactions between First Nations and colonial cultures are conceptualized and discussed. *The Impact of the White Man* is now a historical record in itself: a benchmark for understanding the profound changes that have taken place in our understanding of the topic over half a century. At the same time, it remains a useful source of information for researchers, students and the general public.

This edition includes a table of First Nations names with two maps (Appendix 2), added in 1997 to update the terminology of the 1960s. Some of these spellings have changed again and will, no doubt, continue to be modified as First Nations replace colonial usages with indigenous names and spellings.

As explained on the next page, Duff and the museum intended this as the first volume in a series, an immense task that we would not presume to undertake today. The histories of First Nations in this region are now being investigated in many media and from a variety of perspectives, most importantly by First Nations people who are changing our understanding of our province's troubled colonial past.

Martha Black, Ph.D.
Curator of Ethnology, Royal BC Museum
January 2014

Foreword to the 1992 Edition

The Indian History of British Columbia was proposed as a handbook series in 1960 by Wilson Duff, when he was Curator of Anthropology at the British Columbia Provincial Museum. Duff then undertook to write the series. Volume 1: *The Impact of the White Man* was published in 1964. Two other volumes, "The Southern Kwakiutl", the first of the ethnic histories, and "The First Hundred Centuries", the archaeology of British Columbia, were in preparation when Duff left the Museum in 1965 to take a teaching position at the University of British Columbia. These manuscripts remain unpublished.

The Impact of the White Man has stood the test of time due largely to Duff's rigorous scholarship. He linked historical and ethnographic data long before the practice became academically fashionable. Duff was also an applied scholar. His appearance as an expert witness in the Calder Case, the Nisga'a court challenge to recognize their aboriginal title, exemplified the fact that he lived his beliefs (see Abbott 1981 for more detail on Duff's life).

In the 28 years since it was first published, *The Impact of the White Man* has become a classic of British Columbia anthropology. Some of the terminology used by Duff, although appropriate at the time, is now dated. The term *Indian*, for example, has been replaced by *First Peoples*, *First Nations* or *aboriginal peoples*. In addition, a number of First Nations communities are correcting their names: Nootka is now Nuu-chah-nulth; Kwakiutl is now Kwakwaka'wakw; Bella Coola is now Nuxalk; Niska is now Nisga'a; Shuswap is now Secwepemc; Kootenay is now Ktunaxa; Kitwancool is now Gitanyow; and Nitinat is now Ditidaht. During the period of transition, the usage of these names has become inconsistent in both the aboriginal and the non-aboriginal communities. It is important, however, for the reader of this and other older studies to recognize and respect the new names.*

This volume is being reprinted as a historic piece, not as a contemporary view; consequently, name changes have not been incorporated. A selected guide to further reading has been added to update the original bibliography (see Suggested Reading). It is important to recognize that aboriginal peoples are becoming increasingly critical of studies by non-aboriginal academics. In their views, outsiders cannot adequately understand their cultures and, therefore, do not represent First Nations perspectives of history. In response, First Peoples are writing their own histories to balance the voices of the academics. Some of these works are listed in Suggested Reading.

Richard I. Inglis
Head of Anthropology
Royal British Columbia Museum
1992

---

*   Note for the new edition: See Appendix 2 for a list of First Nations names, as of this printing.

Acknowledgements

I owe debts of gratitude to many people for assistance in preparing this publication. For the redrawing of the maps and charts I am especially indebted to the Geographic Division of the Department of Lands, Forests, and Water Resources. In preparing the chapter on population I received a great deal of assistance from Mr Len Hole of the Division of Vital Statistics, and also from officials of the Indian Affairs Branch. To make a start on a series of publications like this is an easy and normal part of a curator's work, but to bring it to completion is another matter, and often involves the theft of time from family activities. For their co-operation and understanding I extend grateful thanks to my wife, Marion, and my children, Marilyn and Tom.

Wilson Duff, 1965

Preparing for a potlatch in Alert Bay, 1900. "The return of a messenger from Karlokwis. The tribe have accepted the invitation to a potlatch." – C.F. Newcombe. Photo: C.F. Newcombe. RBCM PN842

Introduction

This is the first of a series of volumes on the Indian history of British Columbia, a history that began at least a hundred centuries before the province itself was born, and is still being made. This first volume covers the post-contact or historic period, roughly the past two centuries. It offers a detailed classification of the Indian tribes and bands of the province, a summary of their population trends from early historic times to the present, and an account of the changes that have taken place in the Indian ways of life since the arrival and settlement of Europeans. The past two centuries have been revolutionary ones for the Indian people. Patterns of life that evolved slowly over millennia have been swept aside or forced into radical change. The original inhabitants have been confronted with the necessity of finding a place in the new civilization that outsiders have imposed on their old land. They have had to change, and change a great deal. But they have not yet entirely merged with the newcomers and lost their identity as Indians. Their history will have future chapters still to be written.

Before going further, we should dwell for a moment on the terms "history" and "prehistory", because their meanings can be somewhat confusing. The definition of "prehistory" rests upon the definition of "history", and unfortunately that word is given different meanings in different contexts. In the broad sense, as in "culture history" or "geological history", it is used for any account of past developments. But in the more technical sense used by historians, it means an account of the past based on information from written documents. The prehistory of an area is, therefore, an account of what happened there before it began to be mentioned in written records; in our area, prehistoric times did not end and historic times begin until the 1770s. The aim of the prehistorian, broadly speaking, is the same as that of the historian: to describe past peoples, past ways of life and past events. Another term for prehistoric is "precontact", and for historic is "postcontact". "Protohistoric" refers to the period of late prehistoric time just before the first arrival of Europeans. "Ethnohistory" is a term used for the description of native life and events in early historic times, making use of written records. "Ethnography" is the description of native cultures based on observation and native testimony, and "ethnology" is the study and interpretation of ethnography. "Archaeology" is the study of the material remains of past peoples and cultures, and can be used to shed light on both prehistory and history.

Despite the view that the Indian history of British Columbia is all one story, it is convenient to divide it into two main periods: historic and prehistoric. The information for the historic period is so complete that it permits both a general account and detailed tribal histories. The information for the prehistoric period is not only less complete, it is of a different character. The prehistorian has a different focus on the past. He cannot follow the fortunes of individuals or specific groups of people, but can only trace general developments of language, culture and physical type. He slips into a different scale of time, in which many developments cannot be dated and must be left "floating in time", or can be dated only in relation to other developments, and where the units of time, when they can be determined, are not years, but centuries or even millennia. The second volume in this series will cover the prehistoric period – the first hundred centuries. It will describe the prehistory of the Indians as revealed by their languages, cultures, and physical types, and by archaeology. The remaining volumes will describe the tribes of different sections of the province within historic times: their identities, territories, populations and tribal histories.

At the time of contact, the Indians of this area were among the world's most distinctive peoples. Fully one-third of the native population of Canada lived here. They were concentrated most heavily along the coastline and the main western rivers, and in these areas they developed their cultures to higher peaks, in many respects, than in any other part of the continent north of Mexico. Here, too, was the greatest linguistic diversity in the country, with two dozen languages spoken, belonging to seven of the eleven language families represented in Canada. The coastal tribes were in some ways different from all other American Indians. Their languages, true enough, were members of American families, and physically they were American Indians, though with decided traits of similarity to the peoples of northeastern Asia. Their cultures, however, had a pronounced Asiatic tinge, evidence of basic kinship and long-continued contact with the peoples around the north Pacific rim. Most of all, their cultures were distinguished by a local richness and originality, the product of vigorous and inventive people in a rich environment.

It is not correct to say that the Indians did not own the land but only roamed over the face of it and used it. The patterns of ownership and utilization that they imposed upon the lands and waters were different from those recognized by our system of law, but were nonetheless clearly defined and mutually respected. Even if they didn't subdivide and cultivate the land, they did recognize ownership of plots used for village sites, fishing places, berry and root patches, and similar purposes. Even if they didn't subject the forests to wholesale logging, they did establish ownership of tracts used for hunting, trapping and food-gathering. Even if they didn't sink mine shafts into the mountains, they did own peaks and valleys for Mountain Goat hunting and as sources of raw materials. Except for barren and inaccessible areas that are not utilized even today, every part of the province was formerly within the owned and recognized territory of one or other of the Indian tribes.

The maritime fur-traders treated the Indians as a force to be respected, and found them to be shrewd businessmen who took advantage of the trade in order to develop their cultures further along their own distinctive lines. Had it not been for the ravages of several decades of introduced diseases, alcohol and gunpowder, they would have been a greater force when the settlers began to arrive. The Indians were numerous, but not preponderantly so, and they were uncertain, sick and rapidly declining in numbers. Settlement was not achieved without some friction, but it was achieved without resort to Indian wars. The Indians, it seemed obvious, were bound to disappear. Justice dictated that they should be treated as humanely as possible, but social science had not yet reached the point where it could solve the problems of people in such a plight.

The period of decline is now over, and has been for a generation. The Indian citizens of British Columbia are now rapidly increasing in number, and their leadership and sense of Indian identity are strengthening rather than weakening. Today they form only 2.5 per cent of the population of the province. With increasing intermarriage the definition of "Indian" is passing from the racial to the legal realm, and culturally, only remnants of the old Indian ways of life survive. But in spite of that they still form a distinct ethnic group within the larger society, and most of them still live in separate communities that are different in some respects from non-Indian communities. Some outsiders are disappointed that the Indians have preserved so little of their cultural heritage. Others blame them for not having advanced to full equality with the whites; that is, for not having gained control in a couple of generations of a highly complex way of life that took Europeans many centuries to evolve, and is changing so rapidly that many non-Indians too are being left behind. Their present situation, generally somewhat depressed and between two ways of life, should not be used to judge either their past cultures or their capabilities for the future. Nor is it fair or correct to speak of "the Indian problem", because the situation is not entirely of their own making. The causes of the problem and the responsibility for its solution rest as much with the descendants of the invaders as with the descendants of the original inhabitants. Our common society has unfinished business: old grievances to be settled, unhealthy attitudes to be corrected, and much constructive economic and social development to be accomplished. I hope this volume will help in some measure, by bringing the situation into clearer focus.

The Indians of British Columbia

THE PROBLEM OF INDIAN NAMES

Anyone who speaks or writes about the Indian tribes is immediately faced with the perplexing problem of how to pronounce and write down Indian names. The Indian languages use many sounds that are unfamiliar to a speaker of English, and it soon becomes apparent that our tongues and our alphabet are quite unfitted for the accurate reproduction of Indian words. We have two problems to solve. One is to establish English spellings of Indian names, which, though admittedly imprecise, are nevertheless acceptable. The other is to devise a system of phonetic symbols that can be used to transcribe the Indian sound systems with precision.

Strictly speaking there is no one correct English spelling of an Indian name. In some instances a single form becomes established by usage and general acceptance, but in most cases we find a number of alternative spellings in use. The Indian Affairs Branch may give a sort of unofficial approval to one form (for example, Kwawkewlth), while at the same time the consensus of anthropologists and other writers favours another (Kwakiutl). The Canadian Board on Geographic Names may give its official approval to one or the other, or even to some different form. Then who is to say that one form is more correct than another? In many instances the same Indian name has appeared in the writings of

17

explorers, traders, missionaries, agents and others spelled in a bewildering variety of ways (for example, Euclataw, Yuculta, Yaculta, Lekwiltok, Laycooltach and many more). Though we cannot point to a single correct spelling, we can in most cases choose the one best suited for our purpose. In publications such as this one I have chosen the forms I judge to have become most firmly established, and in cases where no form has become established I have used the simplest spelling that gives a reasonably close approximation of the Indian pronunciation. In quoting earlier sources (as, for example, in the long table of band names that begins on page 27), I retain the spellings they have used.

This is not the place for a detailed discussion of phonetics; however, a few brief comments will help to illustrate the difficulties that English speakers and Indians both face in coping with each other's languages. The human vocal apparatus is capable of producing 200 or more distinct sounds. No one language uses more than three or four dozen of these, and no two languages use exactly the same selection. The meaningful sounds used in language are called phonemes; words are constructed of clusters of phonemes.

Many phonemes used in Indian languages are so different from those used in English that it is difficult for us, without special training, to pronounce (or hear) them correctly. The same problem in reverse causes just as much trouble for the Indians. Anyone whose first language is an Indian one has difficulty with some English sounds. For example, the r sound is foreign to them: for "red" they tend to say "led". They also lack f and v (except for the now-extinct Tsetsaut language), and often substitute the closest equivalents p and b. For some time I carried in my notebook what I thought was the native name for Yale, *Pochail*, before I realized that my informant had been saying "Fort Yale".

The Indian languages do not usually distinguish between s and *sh*, but use a single sound intermediate between the two. When they use this phoneme in English speech, it sounds to us as though they are saying "fiss" instead of "fish", or "yesh" instead of "yes". We have difficulty with Indian sounds that are just slightly different from their English equivalents, because we hear the sounds we have been conditioned to hear. When an

Indian uses the intermediate *s*, we perceive it either as *s* or *sh*. When he uses a phoneme intermediate between our *g* and *k*, we hear it as one or the other: the names Kispiox and Gitksan actually begin with the same phoneme.

Some Indian phonemes are present in European languages other than English. The sound used by a Scot when he says *"loch"* or a German when he says *"ach"* is very common in the local Indian languages, as is the related sound made farther forward in the mouth, as in German *"ich"*. One would therefore expect a Scot to transcribe Indian names more accurately, in some respects, than an Englishman, and that did happen: Dr W. F. Tolmie wrote "Kyumuchkwetoch" for the name that we now write "Kimsquit". The Welsh also share a phoneme with many Indian languages: the surd (unvoiced) *l*, which is pronounced like the *thl* in athlete, except that it is unvoiced (whispered) and slurred into a single sound with the tongue held in the *l* position. Sometimes Indian languages distinguish between two sounds that we consider one and the same. To us the *p* in "ping-pong" is the same phoneme as the *p* in "dip net", although they are, in fact, different sounds. In many Indian languages they would serve as two phonemes.

Coastal Indian languages use many more phonemes in the *g-k* series than does English. English uses only *g* and *k*, and the labialized or rounded forms g^w and k^w. Indian languages use: *g* (a soft *g* made farther back in the throat), *g* (or else ɢ, the intermediate sound between *g* and *k*), g^w (as in "Gwen"), g^y (as in "big-year"), *k* (as in "king"), k^w (as in "quince"), k^y (as in "thank-you"), *k'* (a glottalized or more explosive *k*), k'^w, k'^y, *q* (like *k* but made farther back in the throat), *q'*, q^w, *x* (as in German *"ich"*), and *x̱* (as in German *"ach"*). They also use a more elaborate *l* series than does English: *l* (as in English), *l'* (glottalized, as though forced out through a tightened throat that is suddenly relaxed), ɬ (surd *l*, described above), λ (like *dl* run together), ƛ (*t* and ɬ run together), and *ƛ'* (glottalized ƛ, which can be one of the most explosive of human sounds) .

A further and somewhat more technical discussion of the phonemes used in Indian languages and a phonetic key are given in Appendix 1.

THE CLASSIFICATION OF INDIAN GROUPS

MAJOR ETHNIC DIVISIONS

On an ethnological map that attempts to reduce the complexity of Indian groupings to a workable number of descriptive units, the major ethnic groups can theoretically be drawn on the basis of physical type, culture or language. But it became apparent long ago that, of these, the most convenient criterion is language. The people of two neighbouring bands or villages usually look alike and share similar customs, because physical types and cultures tend to merge imperceptibly with those found in surrounding areas. But if they speak different languages, one can draw a neat line on the map between them. Therefore the larger units on ethnological maps are usually drawn on the basis of language.

For British Columbia the broad classification we shall follow is basically a linguistic one. In this division, which has gained acceptance by long usage, the Indians of the province fall into ten major ethnic groups:

1. Haida.
2. Tsimshian.
3. Kwakiutl.
4. Nootka.
5. Bella Coola.
6. Coast Salish.
7. Interior Salish.
8. Kootenay.
9. Athapaskan.
10. Inland Tlingit.

Each of these groups comprises the speakers of one language or a number of related languages, occupying a continuous area and sharing a basically similar culture. But the system is, admittedly, somewhat illogical and inconsistent. The groups are not linguistically equivalent units; for example, Nootka and Kwakiutl

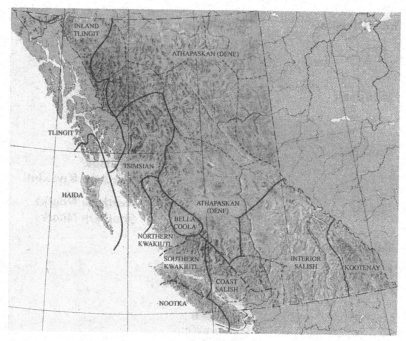

Map 1. Indians of British Columbia: Major Ethnic Divisions

are more closely related to each other than are some of the languages included under the single heading Coast Salish, and Bella Coola, which on purely linguistic grounds should be included with the Coast Salish, is given a separate place because of its location and distinct culture. These ten divisions have been called several things: tribes, nations, speech-communities and other more or less inappropriate terms. "Tribe" conveys a false impression of some degree of internal organization, and is a word better reserved for the smaller local groupings. "Nation" also implies a degree of political organization that did not exist. The Indians had no terms for these major subdivisions; they were vaguely aware of the other people who shared their language, and usually included them with themselves in the term meaning "people", but felt no particular bond of kinship or loyalty to them all. We shall refer to these groups as major ethnic divisions (see Map 1).

Table 1: Indians of British Columbia: Linguistic Subdivisions

Ethnic Division	Language	Dialect
Haida	Haida	**Masset** **Skidegate**
Tsimshian	Tsimshian	**Tsimshian** **Gitksan** **Niska**
Kwakiutl	Kwakiutl	**Haisla** **Heiltsuk** **Southern Kwakiutl**
Nootka	Nootka	**Northern Nootka** **Southern Nootka**
Bella Coola	**Bella Coola**	
Coast Salish	**Comox** **Pentlatch** (extinct) **Sechelt** **Squamish** **Halkomelem** **Straits Salish**	
Interior Salish	**Thompson** **Lillooet** **Shuswap** Okanagon	**Okanagan** **Lakes** (extinct in Canada)
Kootenay	**Kootenay**	
Athapaskan	**Chilcotin** **Carrier** **Sekani** **Tahltan** **Kaska** **Slave** **Beaver** **Tsetsaut** (extinct) **Nicola** (extinct)	
Inland Tlingit	**Tlingit**	

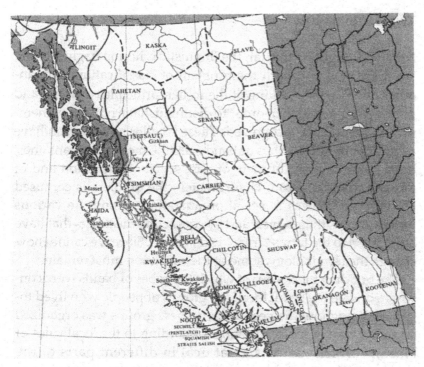

Map 2. Indians of British Columbia: Linguistic Subdivisions.
The names in capitals are languages (Tsetsaut, Pentlatch and Nicola are extinct); the other names are major dialects. (See also Map 7 in Appendix 2.)

LINGUISTIC SUBDIVISIONS

The linguistic criterion may be used to carry our classification one step further, because almost all of the major ethnic divisions may be further subdivided into groups that share single languages or major dialects and form convenient and meaningful regional and cultural units. At this step, too, the division is somewhat arbitrary and inconsistent, and the groups listed are not exactly equivalent in all respects (no system of classification would achieve that). Nor were these groups functioning social or political units, although their members usually recognized that they all shared the same language, culture and territory. But at this level of classification, these linguistic subdivisions form the most meaningful descriptive units.

TRIBES AND BANDS

Having brought us this far, the linguistic criterion begins to fail. We must now approach the problem of classification from another direction, by looking at the Indian principles of social and political organization in order to distinguish the units they themselves created and recognized. These smaller units, which have usually been called tribes or bands, are the most important ones, both from the point of view of past social organization and of present administration. Unfortunately the problem is confused by wide differences in social organization among the various Indian groups themselves, and by conflicting meanings that have been given to the terms "tribe" and "band". Since we cannot now change the terminology, some of the confusion must remain.

The building blocks out of which the tribes or bands were constructed were the small localized groups of people who lived together throughout the year. Each of these groups was organized around a core of kinfolk (defined according to the local rules of kinship, which varied a great deal in different parts of the province). These were the groups that owned the resource areas (though concepts of ownership also varied widely). Where the way of life was nomadic, these groups were small migratory hunting bands. Where life tended to be more sedentary, they were intimately associated with definite localities and village sites, and in many cases were named from these places. In some areas these tiny groups remained autonomous; the Sekani bands, for example, did not join with others to form larger social units. In other areas they retained so high a degree of autonomy that such larger groupings as did form had little functional significance; this was the case among some of the Coast and Interior Salish. But in most areas the ties of kinship and contiguity were extended to form larger aggregations that were recognized and named, and had some functions and some degree of internal organization. These larger aggregations are the ones most properly called tribes.

On the northern coast, where kinship ties were most rigidly defined, matrilineal households or lineages were the basic units that united in each locality to form tribal groups, which usually assembled for part of the year in a common village. Among the Tsimshian these tribes hardened into firmly knit political units (this was somewhat less the case among the Gitksan, Niska and Northern Kwakiutl); but among the Haida they were uneasy and unstable alliances of essentially independent kinship groups, and did not even have collective names other than those of the villages they shared. On the central coast, local bilateral kinship groups likewise clustered themselves into named tribes that shared a village for part of the year. Among the Kwakiutl especially, their internal organization was structured on the principle of rank. Among the Northern Nootka, this organization was carried a step further to form local confederacies of tribes. The entire Coast Salish area was bound together by a diffuse web of bilateral kinship ties; such "tribes" as did exist consisted of clusters of villages that were so closely identified with each other by virtue of locality, dialect, culture and intermarriage that they came to be considered as units distinct enough to bear a common name. The Nanaimo tribe, for example, consisted of five such village units. On the Plateau, the Interior Salish villages tended to be grouped into larger units that have been called bands (Ray 1939, pp. 14-15). Thus the Lake Band of Lillooet is somewhat the equivalent of a Nanaimo tribe of the coast. Among the Kootenay and Athapaskans, on the other hand, the bands were the smaller nomadic groups equivalent to the village units of sedentary peoples, and they tended to remain autonomous and not coalesce into larger units. The Carrier and Tahltan spent part of the year in large groups congregated at good fishing places, and were influenced by the example of their coastal neighbours; consequently they formed aggregations that were equivalent to the tribes of the coast and the bands of the Plateau; in the case of the Carrier these have been called subtribes.

In the long table that follows (Table 2), these aggregations that have been called tribes, bands and subtribes (and for which it would be preferable to reserve the exclusive use of the term "tribe") are shown in the column, "Tribes and Bands, 1850".

We must also take account of the band system of the Indian Affairs Branch, for, in addition to the meanings given above, the word "band" now has a fixed legal meaning for purposes of

Indian administration. In laying out reserves and in other dealings with the Indians, the government was forced to recognize the effective local groups. The first complete and systematic listing of them all is found in the report of the Reserve Commission of 1913-16. For these groups the commissioners often used the words "tribe" and "band" indiscriminately, but in many cases they used them with considerable discernment, with tribes being the larger units, of which bands formed parts. One column of Table 2 is used to show these designations, in relation to the aboriginal group out of which it came and the present band to which it now corresponds. The names in the last column are the accepted names and present populations of the present official bands.

There were some incipient or tentative groupings of tribes into larger units. In some cases, clusters of closely related tribes bore collective names; for example, Cowichan, Saanich, Heiltsuk, Euclataw, Stalo and Babine. In other cases, such a cluster was acknowledged to be closely interrelated but had no joint name; for example, the Haida of Cumshewa, Skedans and Tanoo. A number of descriptive names for regional groups have appeared in print so often that they have become established by usage; for example, Upper Thompson, Lower Kootenay, Northern Kwakiutl and Coast Tsimshian. Though not native names, these have been included in the table. These larger groupings had no internal organization, with two interesting exceptions. After the establishment of Fort Rupert the Southern Kwakiutl tribes arranged themselves in a definite order of rank in order to control their ceremonial relations and potlatching organization, and after the establishment of Port Simpson the nine Lower Skeena Tsimshian tribes did much the same thing.

Table 2: British Columbia Indian Tribes and Bands, 1850-1963.

ETHNIC DIVISION Language Dialect/Regional Group	Tribes and Bands (1850)	Name Given by Reserve Commission (1916)	Present Band Name and Population (1963)
HAIDA			
Haida			
MASSET DIALECT *Masset Inlet:*	Etawas Kayang Yan	Massett Tribe	Masset 903
North Coast:	Kiusta and Kung Dadens Yaku		
SKIDEGATE DIALECT *Skidegate Inlet and West Coast:*	Cathlingskun Skidegate Chaatl ⎱ Haina 1870-98 Kaisun ⎰	Skidegate Tribe	Skidegate 321
Moresby Island:	Cumshewa Skedans Tanoo (New Clew, 1885-97)		
Kunghit Haida:	Ninstints		

ETHNIC DIVISION Language Dialect/Regional Group	Tribes and Bands (1850)	Name Given by Reserve Commission (1916)	Present Band Name and Population (1963)	
TSIMSHIAN Tsimshian TSIMSHIAN *Coast Tsimshian:*				
	Kitasoo (at Kitasoo)	Kitasoo or China Hat Tribe or Band (at Klemtu)	Kitasoo	225
	Kitkiata (at Kitkiata)	Kitkahta (Hartley Bay Tribe) (at Hartley Bay)	Hartley Bay	281
	Kitkatla	Kitkatla Tribe or Band	Kitkatla	613
Lower Skeena Tsimshian: (Port Simpson) In 1887, about 800 of this group founded New Metlakatla, Alaska.	Gitwilgyots Gitzaklalth Gitsees Ginakangeek Ginadoiks Gitandau Gispakloats Gilutsau Gitlan	Tsimpsean Tribe: Port Simpson Band Metlakatla Band Lakelse Tribe or Band (Killutsal)	Port Simpson Metlakatla	1,049 187
Canyon Tsimshian:	Kitsumkalum	Kitsumkaylum Tribe or Band (at Kisumkalum and Port Essington)	Kitsumkalum	102

GITKSAN	Kitselas (at Kitselas Canyon)	Kitselas Tribe (at New Kitselas and Port Essington)	Kitselas	86
	Kitwanga	Kitwangar Tribe / Andimaul Tribe	Kitwanga	283
	Kitwancool	Kitwancool Tribe	Kitwancool	201
	Kitsegukla	Kitsegukla Tribe	Kitsegukla	309
	Kitanmaks	Hazelton Tribe: Getanmax Band	Hazelton	583
	Kispiox	Kispaiox Tribe: Glen Vowell Band	Kispiox / Glen Vowell	432 / 159
	Kisgegas	Kisgegas Tribe	(amalgamated with Hazelton)	
	Kuldo	Kuldoe Tribe	(amalgamated with Kispiox)	
NISKA	Gitkateen (at Gitiks, Kwunwoq, Angida, Gitlakaus)	Nass River (Nishga) Tribe: Kincolith Band / Lachkaltsap Band (at Greenville)	Kincolith / Lakalzap	678 / 551
	Gitgigenik (at Andegulay)			
	Gitwunksithk	Kitwilluchsilt Band	Canyon City	116

ETHNIC DIVISION Language Dialect/Regional Group	Tribes and Bands (1850)	Name Given by Reserve Commission (1916)	Present Band Name and Population (1963)
NISKA (cont.)	Gitlakdamiks	Kitladamax Band Aiyansh Band	Gitlakdamix 620
KWAKIUTL **Kwakiutl** NORTHERN KWAKIUTL *Haisla Dialect:*	Haisla (Kitamaat)	Kitimat Tribe or Band	Kitamaat 721
	Kemano (Kitlope)	Kitlope Tribe or Band	
Heiltsuk Dialect:	Haihais	(with Kitasoo Tsimshian)	
	Istitoch Oyalitoch Owitlitoch Koksyitoch	Bella Bella Tribe	Bella Bella 970
		Kokyet Tribe	
	Owikeno	Owekano Tribe (at Katit)	Oweekano (at Rivers Inlet) 132
SOUTHERN KWAKIUTL	Gwasilla (at Wyclese, Smith Inlet)	Quawshelah Tribe (at Takush Harbour)	Quawshelah 128

Nakwoktak (at Kequesta, Nugent Sound)	Nahkwockto Tribe or Band (at Blunden Harbour)	Nakwakto	61
Gwawaenuk (at Watson Island)	Gilford Island Tribe: Kwawwawineuch Band	Kwawwaineuk (Watson Island)	16
Hahuamis (on Wakeman Sound)	Gilford Island Tribe: Ahkwawahmish Band (at Gwayasdums)	(with Kwiksootainuk)	
Kwiksootainuk (at Gwayasdums)	(error) Village Island Tribe: Kwicksitaneau Band (at Village Island)	Gilford Island (at Gwayasdums)	192
Tsawatainuk (on Kingcome River)	Gilford Island Tribe: Tsahwawtineuch Band (at Gwayasdums)	Tsawataineuk (Kingcome River)	262
Tenaktak (at Wahkash on Knight Inlet)	Knight Inlet Tribe: Tanockteuch Band (at Harbledown Island)	Tenakteuk (Harbledown Island)	102
Awaetlala (at Hanwadi, Knight Inlet)	Knight Inlet Tribe: Ahwaheettlala Band (at Harbledown Island)		
Mamalilikulla (at Village Island)	Village Island Tribe: Mahmalilikullah Band	Mamalilikulla (Village Island)	127

ETHNIC DIVISION

Language Dialect/Regional Group	Tribes and Bands (1850)	Name Given by Reserve Commission (1916)	Present Band Name and Population (1963)
SOUTHERN KWAKIUTL (cont.)	Matilpi (Maamtagila) (at Etsekin)	Mahteelthpe Tribe	(joined Tlawitsis)
	Tlawitsis (at Kalokwis on Turnour Island)	Turnour Island Tribe or Band	Turnour Island 146
	Nimpkish (at Cheslakees, Nimpkish River)	Nimkeesh Tribe (at Alert Bay)	Nimpkish 686
Fort Rupert tribes:	Kwakiutl	Kwawkewlth Tribe: Kwawkewlth Band Kwiahkah Band	Kwawkewlth (at Fort Rupert) 208
	Kweeha		
	Walas Kwakiutl	Walaskwawkewlth Band	
	Komkiutis		
Nahwitti tribes:	Tlatlasikwala Nakumgilisala Yutlinuk (at Nahwitti)	Nahwitti Tribe or Band (on Hope Island)	Nuwitti (at Quatsino and Fort Rupert) 20

Quatsino Sound tribes:	Quatsino Tribe:		
Koskimo (at Quattishe)	Koskemo Band (at Quattishe)		
Quatsino (on Forward Inlet)	Quastino Band (at Winter Harbour)	Quatsino (at Quattishe)	88
Giopino (on Koprino Harbour)	Klaskino Tribe (one man, at Quattishe)		
Klaskino (Klaskino Inlet)			
Euclataw tribes	Laichkwiltach Tribe:		
Weewiakay (Cape Mudge after 1860)	Wewayakay Band	Cape Mudge	285
Weewiakum (Campbell River after 1860)	Wewayakum Band	Campbell River	154
Kweeha (Phillips Arm)	Kwiahkah Band	Kwiakah	6
Tlaaluis (Arran Rapids)	Kahkahmatsis Band		
Hahamatsees (Salmon River)			
NOOTKA			
Nootka			
NORTHERN NOOTKA:			
Chickliset	Checkleset Tribe (at Acous)	(joined Kyuquot)	
Kyuquot	Kyoquot Tribe (at Village Island)	Kyuquot	158
Ehatisat	Esperanza Tribe: Ehatsaht Band (at Oke)	Ehattesaht (at Queens Cove)	78

ETHNIC DIVISION Language Dialect/Regional Group	Tribes and Bands (1850)	Name Given by Reserve Commission (1916)	Present Band Name and Population (1963)
NORTHERN NOOTKA (cont.)	Nuchatlet	Esperanza Tribe: Nuchatlitz Band (at Nuchatl)	Nuchatlaht 72
	Muchalat	Nootka Tribe: Matchilacht Band (at Yuquot)	(joined Nootka)
	Moachat	Nootka Tribe (at Yuquot, Friendly Cove)	Nootka 204
CENTRAL NOOTKA:	Hesquiat	Hesquiat Tribe (at Hesquiat)	Hesquiaht 256 (mostly at Hot Springs Cove)
	Ahousat	Clayoquot Tribe: Ahousat Band (at Marktosis)	Ahousaht 579
	Kelsemat	Clayoquot Tribe: Kelsemart Band (at Yarksis)	(joined Ahousaht)
	Clayoquot	Clayoquot Tribe: Clayoquot Band (at Opitsat)	Clayoquot 265
	Ucluelet	Ucluelet Tribe	Ucluelet 240
	Toquat	Toquart Tribe	Toquaht 64

	Uchucklisat	Uchucklisit Tribe	Uchucklesaht (mostly at Kildonan)	67
	Hopachisat	Opitchisaht Tribe (at Alberni)	Opetchesaht	82
	Tsishaat (Seshart)	Seshart Tribe or Band (at Alberni)	Sheshaht	304
	Ohiat	Ohiet Tribe	Ohiet (at Bamfield and Sarita)	208
SOUTHERN NOOTKA:	Nitinat	Nitinat Tribe (at Clo-oose)	Nitinaht	211
	Pachenat	Pacheena Tribe (at Port Renfrew)	Pacheenaht	111
BELLA COOLA **Bella Coola**	Bella Coola (several villages along the Bella Coola River)	Bella Coola Tribe	Bella Coola	536
	Kimsquit (several villages on the Dean and Kimsquit rivers)	Kemsquit Tribe	(joined Bella Coola)	
	Talio (several villages on South Bentinck Arm)	(joined Bella Coola)		

ETHNIC DIVISION Language Dialect/Regional Group	Tribes and Bands (1850)	Name Given by Reserve Commission (1916)	Present Band Name and Population (1963)	
COAST SALISH Comox *Comox*	Several tribes that, before 1850, lived in the Quadra Island area; the remnants were driven south to Comox by the Euclataw.	Comox Tribe	Comox	79
Homathko	Homathko	Homalco Tribe (at Church House)	Homalco	216
Sliammon	Sliammon	Sliammon Tribe or Band (near Powell River)	Sliammon	347
Klahuse	Klahuse	Klahoose Tribe or Band (at Squirrel Cove)	Klahoose	92
Sechelt *Sechelt*	Sechelt	Seshelt Tribe or Band	Sechelt	428
Pentlatch (extinct) *Pentlatch*	Before 1850, three groups lived on Comox Harbour, Denman Island and Englishman River.	(joined Comox)		

Group	Villages	Tribe / Band	Band	Population
		Qualicum Tribe (a small new mixed group)	Qualicum	35
Squamish *Squamish*	A large number of villages on the Squamish River and Howe Sound. Burrard Inlet shared with Musqueam.	Squamish Tribe: Kowtain Band, Seichem Band, Yookwitz Band, Cheakamus Band, Kapilano Band, Burrard Inlet Band	Squamish (at Squamish River, Capilano and North Vancouver)	955
			Burrard	123
Halkomelem *Nanaimo*	Nanaimo (five villages on Nanaimo Harbour and the Nanaimo River)	Nanaimo Tribe	Nanaimo	456
	Nanoose (Nanoose Harbour)	Nanoose Tribe	Nanoose	70
Chemainus	Chemainus (Kulleet Bay) Sicameen (Ladysmith Harbour) Halalt (Willy Island)	Chemainus Tribe: Chemainus Band, Siccameen Band (including Kumalockasun Band), Halalt Band	Chemainus	366
			Halalt (Westholme)	95

ETHNIC DIVISION Language Dialect/Regional Group	Tribes and Bands (1850)	Name Given by Reserve Commission (1916)	Present Band Name and Population (1963)
Chemainus (cont.)	Lyacksun (Shingle Point)	Lyacksun Band	Lyacksun (Westholme) 77
	Penelakuts (Kuper Island)	Penelakut Band	Penelakut 326
		(included Tsussie)	
	Yekoloas	(joined Penelakuts)	
	(Telegraph Harbour)		
	Lilmalche (Lamalchi Bay)	(joined Penelakuts)	
Cowichan	Cowichan Lake	Cowichan Lake Tribe	Cowichan Lake 4
	Somenos (Cowichan River)	Cowichan Tribe	Cowichan 1,228
	Quamichan	(amalgamation in 1888 of:	
	(lower Cowichan River)	Somenos, Quamichan,	
	Comiaken	Comiaken,	
	(lower Cowichan River)	Clemclemaluts,	
	Clemclemaluts	Koksilah, Kenipsen	
	(lower Cowichan River)	and Kilpaulus)	
	Koksilah (Koksilah River)		
	Kenipsen (Cowichan Bay)		
	Kilpaulus (Cowichan Bay)		
	Malahat	(considered part of Saanich	89
	(southernmost	Tribe)	
	Halkomelem group)		

		Tsawwassen Tribe	Tsawwassen	
Stalo (along the Fraser River from the mouth to 8 km above Yale)	Tsawwassen	Tsawwassen Tribe	Tsawwassen	56
	Musqueam	Musqueam Tribe or Band	Musqueam	302
	Kwantlen	Langley Tribe or Band	Langley	77
	Whonnock	(part of Langley)		
	Coquitlam	Coquitlam Tribe or Band	Coquitlam	24
	Katzie	Katzie Tribe	Katzie	153
	Matsqui	Matsqui Tribe or Band	Matsqui	38
	Sumas	Sumass Tribe: Sumass Band	Sumas-Kilgard	71
	Nicomen	Lakahahmen-Nicomeen Band	Sumas-Lakahahmen	95
	Chilliwack	Chilliwack Tribe: Aitchelitz Band	Aitchelitz	6
		Kwawkwawapilt Band	Kwawkwawapilt	8
		Skulkayn Band	Skulkayn	41
		Skwah Band	Skwah	164
		Skway Band	Skway	37
		Soowahlie Band	Soowahlie	110
		Squiala Band	Squiala	36
		Yakweakwioose Band	Yakweakwioose	31
			Tzeachten	106

ETHNIC DIVISION

Language Dialect/Regional Group	Tribes and Bands (1850)	Name Given by Reserve Commission (1916)	Present Band Name and Population (1963)	
Stalo (cont.)	Scowlitz	Harrison River Tribe: Scowlitz Band	Scowlitz	106
	Chehalis	Chehalis Band	Chehalis	325
	Pilalt	Cheam Tribe or Band	Cheam	123
	Tait	Popkum Tribe or Band	Popkum	8
		Squawtits Tribe or Band	Peters	31
	Many villages, not clearly grouped into tribes.	Ohamil Tribe or Band	Ohamil	46
		Skawahlook Tribe or Band	Skawahlook	27
		Hope Tribe or Band	Hope	116
		Yale Tribe:	Yale	61
		Union Bar Band	Union Bar	41
		Seabird Island (a new settlement used by the above six groups in common)	Seabird Island	243
Straits Salish *Saanich*	Tsartlip	Saanich Tribe	Tsartlip (Brentwood Bay)	299
	Paquachin		Pauquachin (Cole Bay)	122

	Tsaykum		Tseycum (Patricia Bay)	61
	Tsaout		Tsawout (East Saanich)	211
Lekwungen	Several villages between Parry Bay and Cordova Bay. They converged on Fort Victoria, and later formed two distinct groups.	Songhees Tribe	Songhees	117
		Esquimalt Tribe	Esquimalt	55
Klallam	Beecher Bay Klallam (moved north across the Juan de Fuca Strait shortly before 1850)	Becher Bay Tribe (Cheerno)	Beecher Bay	73
Sooke	Sooke	Sooke Tribe	Sooke	44
Semiahmoo	Semiahmoo	Semiahmoo Tribe or Band	Semiahmoo (White Rock)	28
INTERIOR SALISH Thompson *Lower Thompson*	Lower Thompson: Many semi-permanent villages along the Fraser River from Spuzzum to 18 km below Lytton.	Spuzzum Tribe or Band Boston Bar Tribe or Band Boothroyd Tribe: Chomok Band	Spuzzum Boston Bar Boothroyd	42 79 123

ETHNIC DIVISION Language Dialect/Regional Group	Tribes and Bands (1850)	Name Given by Reserve Commission (1916)	Present Band Name and Population (1963)	
Upper Thompson	Upper Fraser band: Several villages, 35 to 69 km up the Fraser River from Lytton.	(part of Lytton Tribe)		
	Lytton band: Many villages along the Fraser River and part of Thompson River.	Kanaka Bar Tribe or Band	Kanaka Bar	61
		Siska Flat Tribe or Band	Siska	88
		Skuppah Tribe or Band	Skuppah	15
		Lytton Tribe or Band	Lytton	826
		Nicomen Tribe or Band	Nicomen	37
	Spences Bridge band: Several villages along the Thompson River.	Cook's Ferry Tribe	Cook's Ferry	124
		Oregon Jack Creek Tribe	Oregon Jack	18
		Ashcroft Tribe	Ashcroft	69
	Nicola band: Several villages from 16 km up the Nicola River to the foot of Nicola Lake. Most of this area was formerly Nicola Athapaskan territory.	Lower Nicola Tribe	Lower Nicola	343
			Nooaitch	85
			Shackan	65
		(Coldwater reserves used by Upper and Lower Similkameen, Lower Thompson, Siska, in common.)	Coldwater	240

Lillooet

Lower Lillooet	Lillooet River band: Several villages along the Lillooet River between Harrison and Lillooet lakes.	Douglas Tribe: Douglas Band Skookumchuck Band Samahquam Band	Douglas 100 Skookumchuck 164 Samahquam 96
	Pemberton band: Several villages above Lillooet Lake.	Pemberton Tribe or Band	Mount Currie 768
Upper Lillooet	Lake band: Several villages on Anderson and Seton lakes.	Anderson Lake Tribe or Band Seton Lake Tribe or Band	Anderson Lake 97 Seton Lake 289
	Fraser River band: Several villages along the Fraser River.	Bridge River Tribe or Band Fountain Tribe or Band Cayoosh Creek Tribe or Band Lillooet Tribe or Band	Bridge River 135 Fountain 385 Cayuse Creek 58 Lillooet 88

Shuswap

Fraser River Shuswap	Soda Creek band	Soda Creek Tribe or Band	Soda Creek 118
	Williams Lake band (Sugar Cane)	Williams Lake Tribe or Band	Williams Lake 198

ETHNIC DIVISION Language Dialect/Regional Group	Tribes and Bands (1850)	Name Given by Reserve Commission (1916)	Present Band Name and Population (1963)	
Fraser River Shuswap (cont.)	Alkali Lake band	Alkali Lake Tribe or Band	Alkali Lake	257
	Dog Creek band	Dog Creek Tribe or Band	(joined Canoe Creek)	
	Canoe Creek band	Canoe Creek Tribe or Band	Canoe Creek	228
	High Bar band	High Bar Tribe or Band	High Bar	6
	Clinton band	Clinton Tribe or Band	Clinton	27
Canyon Shuswap	Four bands on the Chilcotin River and Riske Creek; after 1862, smallpox remnants joined the Alkali Lake band.			
Lake Shuswap	Canim Lake band	Canim Lake Tribe or Band	Canim Lake	217
North Thompson Shuswap	Upper North Thompson band Lower North Thompson band	North Thompson and Canoe Lake Tribe	North Thompson	226
Bonaparte Shuswap	Pavilion band	Pavilion Tribe or Band	Pavilion	142
	Bonaparte River band	Bonaparte Tribe	Bonaparte	279

Group	Band	Tribe	Name	Number
Kamloops Shuswap	Ashcroft band (extinct)			
	Deadman's Creek band	Deadman's Creek Tribe	Deadman's Creek	213
	Kamloops band	Kamloops Tribe	Kamloops	313
Shuswap Lake Shuswap	Adams Lake band	Adams Lake Tribe: Sahhaltkum Band	Adams Lake	309
		Neskainlith-Halaut Tribe	Neskainlith	259
	South Thompson band	Little Shuswap Lake Tribe	Little Shuswap	160
	Shuswap Lake band			
	Spallumcheen band	Spallumcheen Tribe	Spallumcheen	306
Arrow Lakes	(see Lakes Okanagan)	Arrow Lake Tribe	(extinct)	
Kinbasket	(Band of mixed Shuswap origin on lower Columbia Lake.)	Shuswap Tribe: Kinbasket's Band	Shuswap	111
Okanagon *Upper (Lake) Okanagan*	Komaplix band	Okanagan Tribe (near Vernon)	Okanagan	774
	Penticton band	Penticton Tribe	Penticton	281
	Douglas Lake band	Upper Nicola Tribe (Douglas and Nicola lakes)	Upper Nicola	341

ETHNIC DIVISION Language Dialect/Regional Group	Tribes and Bands (1850)	Name Given by Reserve Commission (1916)	Present Band Name and Population (1963)	
Upper (Lake) Okanagan (cont.)	Inkameep band	Osoyoos Tribe	Osoyoos	152
Similkameen	Ashnola band	Lower Similkameen Tribe	Lower Similkameen	172
	Upper Similkameen band	Upper Similkameen Tribe	Upper Similkameen	28
"Lakes" (Arrow Lakes) The Arrow Lakes area was occupied by an Okanagon-speaking tribe now centred south of the U.S. border on the Colville Reservation; this area was also shared by Shuswap, Okanagan and Kootenay peoples.		Arrow Lake Tribe (a small mixed group)	(extinct as a definable group)	
KOOTENAY Kootenay *Lower Kootenay*	Creston band	Lower Kootenay Tribe	Lower Kootenay	84
Upper Kootenay	Tobacco Plains band	Kootenay Tribe	Tobacco Plains	63
	Fort Steele band		St Mary's	172
			Columbia Lake	124

ATHAPASKAN

Chilcotin

Several semi-nomadic bands occupying the Chilcotin drainage above Hanceville, Dean River beyond Anahim Lake, and the upper Homathko and Klinaklini rivers. They shifted eastward after 1850.

	Tribe or Band	Band	
	Anaham Tribe or Band	Anaham	503
	Alexis Creek Tribe or Band	Alexis Creek	261
	Nemaiah Valley Tribe or Band	Nemiah Valley	141
	Stone Tribe or Band	Stone	140
	Toosey (Riske Creek) Tribe or Band	Toosey	84

Carrier

Lower Carrier

	Tribe or Band	Band	
Algatcho	Ulkatcho Tribe or Band	Ulkatcho (Anahim Lake)	240
Kluskoten	Kluskus Tribe: Kluskus Band	Kluskus	65
Nazkoten	Kluskus Tribe: Nazco Band Euchinico Band Blackwater Tribe	Nazko	123
Tauten (Talkotin)	Quesnel Tribe or Band	Quesnel	17
	Alexandria Tribe or Band	Alexandria	42

Upper Carrier

	Tribe or Band	Band	
Tanoten	Fort George Tribe or Band	Fort George	67
Tachickwoten Nulkiwoten	Stony Creek Tribe or Band	Stony Creek	328
Cheslatta	Cheslatta Tribe	Cheslatta	98

ETHNIC DIVISION Language Dialect/Regional Group	Tribes and Bands (1850)	Name Given by Reserve Commission (1916)	Present Band Name and Population (1963)
Upper Carrier (cont.)	(small scattered groups)	Francois Lake Tribe: Francois Lake Band Decker Lake Band Maxim Lake Band Skin Tyee Band	Omineca 133
		Francois Lake Tribe: Uncha Lake Band	(joined Cheslatta)
		Francois Lake Tribe: Burns Lake Band	Burns Lake 25
	Necosliwoten	Stuart Lake Tribe: Necoslie Band	Necoslie 418 (Fort St James)
	Tachiwoten	Tatche Tribe: Tatche Band, Pinchie Band, Yacutee Band, Grand Rapids Band, Trembleur Lake Band	Stuart-Trembleur Lake 500 (mostly at Tatche and Fort St James)
	Natliwoten	Fraser Lake Tribe: Fraser Lake Band	Fraser Lake 143
	Stellawoten	Stellaquo Band	Stellaquo 146
		Tatche Tribe: North Takla Lake Band (amalgamated in 1959 with Fort Connelly Band)	Takla Lake 221

Babines	Nataotin (Babine Lake Carrier)	Hagwilget Tribe: Fort Babine Band, Old Fort Babine Band	Lake Babine (mostly at Fort Babine and Burns Lake)	739
	Witsiwoten (Bulkley River Carrier)	Hagwilget Tribe: Moricetown Band	Moricetown	464
			Tsitck (Hagwilget)	170

Sekani

Tseloni

Traded at Fort Nelson until 1910, then most moved west and traded at Lower Post as "Nelson River Nomads".

Fort Nelson Sicannies (not enumerated separately after 1956)   (joined Slave Band)

Nelson River Tribe (in 1960 became part of the Liard River Band)

Sasuchan

Traded at Fort Connelly (Bear Lake). When Fort Grahame was established, ca 1890, about half moved there; a nomadic offshoot of this group, the Otzane or "Fort Grahame Nomads", began to trade at McDames in 1909.

Sicannees Tribe: Fort Grahame Band (later split into Fort Ware and Fort Grahame bands, which amalgamated in 1959)   Finlay River (at Fort Ware and Ingenika River)   222

Fort Grahame Nomads (considered part of Casca Tribe)   (now part of Liard River Band)

ETHNIC DIVISION Language Dialect/Regional Group	Tribes and Bands (1850)	Name Given by Reserve Commission (1916)	Present Band Name and Population (1963)
Sasuchan (cont.)		Bear Lake Tribe (In the 1920s a nomadic group moved to Fort Grahame, then Caribou Hide, and in 1952 reached Telegraph Creek. (The remainder, the Fort Connelly Band, amalgamated in 1959 with North Takla Lake.)	"Bear Lakers" enumerated with the Tahltan; in 1962 moved back to Iskut (Kluachon) Lake.
Yutuwichan			(now part of Takla Lake Band)
Tsekani		Siccanees Tribe: Fort McLeod Band	McLeod Lake 142
Tahltan Five bands centred on Stikine, with territories north to Nahlin and south to the upper Nass River.	Tichaanoteen Tahlagoteen Thlegtodeen (Tlepanoten) Nahlodeen Nassgodeen	Tahltan Tribe or Band (includes, since 1952, the Bear Lakers, now at Iskut Lake)	Tahltan 637 (at Telegraph Creek, Cassiar, Lower Post and elsewhere)

Kaska Several bands on the upper branches of the Liard River.	Dease River Kaska (Tsezotina) Upper Liard Kaska Francis Lake Kaska (Titshotina)	Casca Tribe or Band (McDames Creek) Liard and Francis Lake Tribe or Band (Lower Post)	(Since 1960, part of Liard River Band, numbering 410, many of whom live in the Yukon.)
Slave Several bands, of which only one was in B.C.	Fort Nelson Slave	Fort Nelson Slave	Slave (at Fort Nelson and Prophet River) 268
Beaver Two bands along the Peace River in B.C.	Fort St John Beaver	Fort St John Beaver	Beaver (at Doig River and Blueberry) 168
	Hudson Hope Beaver	Hudson Hope Beaver	Hudson Hope (at Halfway River and West Moberly Lake) 122
		Salteaux (a Cree band that settled at east Moberly Lake in 1910, now mixed with Beaver)	Salteau 125

ETHNIC DIVISION Language Dialect/Regional Group	Tribes and Bands (1850)	Name Given by Reserve Commission (1916)	Present Band Name and Population (1963)
Tsetsaut	An Athapaskan group living on the Iskut, Unuk and upper Nass rivers and adjacent salt-water inlets. The remnants joined the Niska at Kincolith in 1885.	(extinct)	(extinct as a definable group)
Nicola	An Athapaskan group living on the upper Nicola and Similkameen rivers, called Stuwihamuk by the Thompson and Okanagan, who absorbed them by about 1850.	(extinct)	(extinct as a definable group)
INLAND TLINGIT **Tlingit**	About 1850, mixed Tlingits and Athapaskans on the upper Taku River moved north and formed the Atlin and Teslin bands of "Inland Tlingit".	Atlin-Teslin Lake Tribe	Atlin-Teslin 199 (most live in the Yukon)

Population

THE ABORIGINAL POPULATION

POPULATION IN 1835

We would very much like to know how many Indians there were in the 1770s, before the first effects of European contact began to be felt; but unfortunately it is not possible with the information now available to make accurate estimates for any time earlier than 1835. About that time the traders of the Hudson's Bay Company were instructed to make censuses of the tribes with which they were in contact, and several of the resulting counts are available for sections of British Columbia. Some of these are evidently quite accurate, but most are obviously and grossly inaccurate. Nevertheless, when judiciously used and checked one against the others, they do provide a starting point for estimating the populations at the time*. These censuses will be used in greater detail in later volumes, in connection with the histories of the individual tribes. The estimates obtained in this way can be checked by the use of another approach. By starting from the first

---

* They cannot be regarded as precise head counts, as Taylor (1963) has recently assumed.

53

accurate censuses (mostly in the 1880s), and working back in light of what is known about epidemics, wars, and other such occurrences in the intervening period, one can arrive at estimates for 1835. The figures shown in Table 3 result from combining these two approaches.*

POPULATION BEFORE 1835

The population in aboriginal times must have been considerably larger than 70,000. By 1835 the Indians had already been in contact with Europeans for six decades, and introduced diseases, firearms and alcohol must already have taken a substantial toll. We know from native traditions and scattered reports in early journals that a number of areas suffered from smallpox epidemics, but it is difficult to judge whether their effects in any given instance were local or widespread, or to what degree the population had recovered from their effects by 1835. In 1787, for example, Captain Portlock described the effects of a smallpox attack that had occurred some years before among the Tlingit (Beresford 1789, p. 271), and in 1794, Captain Bishop recorded that there had been a severe epidemic some years before at Kaigani, and found the disease actively raging among Chief Shakes and his people at Kitkatla (Bishop 1795, pp. 105, 116). At about the same period other epidemics were sweeping across the central and western parts of the continent, and there is little doubt that their effects reached at least some of the tribes in British Columbia.

One of the most devastating of the early epidemics stopped just short of British Columbia. This was the terrible "intermittent fever" or "ague" that broke out near Fort Vancouver in the lower Columbia River valley in 1830, and in three years wiped out about three-quarters of the native population of that densely inhabited area. It has recently been established that this plague was

---

* Note for the new edition: See Boyd 1990 and 1994, Harris 1994, and their references for more recent analyses of population figures for Northwest Coast First Peoples.

Table 3: British Columbia Indian Population, 1835-1963

Ethnic Division	1835	1885	Low Year	1963
Haida	6,000	800	588 (1915)	1,224
Tsimshian	8,500	4,550	3,550 (1895)	6,475
Kwakiutl	10,700	3,000	1,854 (1929)	4,304
Nootka	7,500	3,500	1,605 (1939)	2,899
Bella Coola	2,003	450	249 (1929)	536
Coast Salish	12,000	5,525	4,120 (1915)	8,495
Interior Salish	13,500	5,800	5,348 (1890)	9,512
Kootenay	1,000	625	381 (1939)	443
Athapaskan	8,800	3,750	3,716 (1895)	6,912
Total for B.C.	70,000	28,000	22,605 (1929)	40,800

malaria (Cook 1955), and fortunately the mosquito that transmits malaria does not seem to extend north as far as British Columbia.

Other writers have been bold enough to guess at what the pre-contact population of the province may have been. Hill-Tout (1907, p. 28) set it at 125,000 or more. The best estimates are those of James Mooney, who attempted to establish the populations in 1780 of all North American tribes (Mooney 1928); his estimates for those within British Columbia give a total of 86,000. All that can be said with confidence is that the aboriginal population must have been at least 80,000, and probably somewhat more.

DENSITY AND DISTRIBUTION

Eighty thousand may not seem a large number, being only 5 per cent of the present population of the province, but for native North America it represented an unusually high density of population. No other region of Canada was so heavily occupied; in fact, about 40 per cent of all the native people in the country lived within the present boundaries of British Columbia. This distribution should be viewed as part of the pattern found on the continent as a whole. Native North Americans, generally speaking, found life on the coastline much more congenial than an agricultural life or a nomadic hunting existence. Of the 1,000,000 native people who lived north of Mexico, about 30 per cent lived along the Pacific coast, on about 6 per cent of the land area. The density in this coastal strip was greatest in the south, diminishing to the north. The agricultural areas of the continent (about 40 per cent of the total) supported populations that were on the average less than half as heavy as the coast, and the remainder supported less than one-tenth as heavy a population (Kroeber 1947, p. 144).

Map 3 shows the distribution pattern in British Columbia in 1835. The heaviest concentration was among the coastal tribes, diminishing from south to north. The heavy concentration extended inland along the lower reaches of the Fraser, Bella Coola, Skeena and Nass rivers, and to a lesser extent into the middle reaches of the Fraser and Skeena systems. Over the divide beyond the Pacific drainage, population fell off sharply. This distribution, it might be said, simply reflects the relative richness of food resources in the different areas. But that would not tell the entire story, because it also reflects the cultural developments by which the people fitted themselves to live in what otherwise would seem a barren and hostile environment. Some areas such as the Queen Charlotte Islands and the outer coasts of Vancouver Island were much more heavily populated then than they are by us today.

CHANGES SINCE 1835

The over-all trend of Indian population since 1835 has been one of rapid decline followed by slow recovery and then increasingly rapid growth. The steep decline that had begun with the first European contacts continued until about 1890; it was checked and reversed by about 1939, and the population has been increasing at a faster and faster rate ever since. This trend is shown on the graph on the facing page.

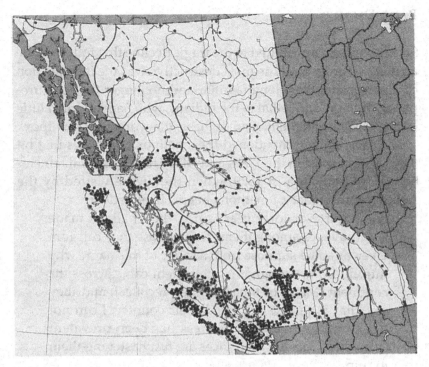

Map 3. Indians of British Columbia: Population Distribution, 1835. One dot represents 100 persons. Populations shown near locations of villages, rather than scattered throughout tribal territories.

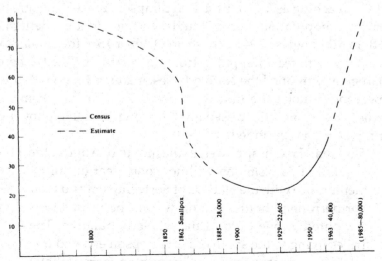

Indians of British Columbia: Population Trend, 1835-1963, and projected to 1985.

Rapid Decline

Several causes contributed to the tragic decline that followed the arrival of Europeans. The most destructive was the introduction of diseases that were long familiar and no longer fatal to Europeans, but new and lethal to the Indians, who had inherited little or no resistance to them. And of these, the worst was smallpox.

We have already mentioned the smallpox epidemics that hit the northern coast in the 1780s and '90s. These were still remembered by the Haida in 1829, when they were visited by the American missionary, Jonathon Green. He recorded:

> Some thirty or forty years since, the smallpox made great ravages among them. This disease they call Tom Dyer, as some suppose from a sailor of this name who introduced it, though it is probable it came across the continent. Many of their old men recollect, and they say, that it almost desolated their country. I can not learn that any general sickness has been prevalent since that time, but their vices are fast hastening them to ruin.

The vices he referred to were wars, intemperance and infanticide of babies born of white fathers (Green 1829, p. 29).

Another destructive epidemic spread down the northern coast in 1836, reaching as far south as Port Simpson, the main centre of Tsimshian population. James Douglas referred to it in a letter in 1838 (in McLoughlin 1941): "Early in October 1836 the small Pox advancing with fearful rapidity from the Northern Coast, where it had greatly thinned the Native Tribes, made its first desolating appearance among the Indians of the Fort." The fur business, needless to say, was depressed all that winter and the following spring. Douglas continued:

> The small Pox disappeared in the month of August: the effects of this visitation will not soon wear out of remembrance with the Natives of Fort Simpson and their northern neighbours, among whom the mortality is computed at one third of the whole population. The Tribes living to the south of Fort Simpson escaped this calamity, which singularly enough appears to have been arrested in its progress at that place.

The village of Yan, near Masset, Queen Charlotte Islands. Like many villages on the coast, Yan was abandoned after the smallpox and other epidemics of the 19th century. C.F. Newcombe photograph, RBCM PN30.

A visitor to the fort in 1845, commenting on this epidemic, noted that its ravages had been "more against the families of the chiefs, than among the inferior classes" (Dunn 1845, p. 410).

The most terrible single calamity to befall the Indians of British Columbia was the smallpox epidemic that started in Victoria in 1862. Unique circumstances caused it to spread faster and farther than any previous outbreak could possibly have done, and within two years it had reached practically all parts of the province, and killed about one-third of the native people.

Following upon the first gold excitement in 1858, it became the habit of many of the northern coastal tribes to visit Victoria in large numbers, and at times more than 2,000 "Hydahs", "Stickeens", "Chimseans", "Bella Bellas", "Fort Ruperts" and so on were camped on the outskirts of the settlement. That was the situation in April 1862 when a white man with smallpox arrived from San Francisco. Before long, despite dire warnings in the *Colonist*, the disease reached the camps of the Indians, and they began to die in fearful numbers. Alarmed, the authorities burned the camps and forced the Indians to leave. They started up the coast for home, taking the disease with them, leaving the infection at every place they touched. The epidemic spread like a forest fire up the coast and into the interior; the details of its progress

Women of Quatsino Sound on northern Vancouver Island, around 1879. In a period of declining population, few children appear in such group photographs. Richard Maynard photograph, RBCM PN2552.

can be followed in dispatches sent to the *Colonist* from Nanaimo, Fort Rupert, Bella Coola, Port Simpson, Stickeen, Lillooet and Williams Lake. At Cape Mudge the Euclataws ambushed a party of Haidas heading home, and caught the disease as part of their spoils. In the Chilcotin. a white man took blankets from the bodies of the dead and sold them to other Indians, who were infected in their turn. At Port Simpson, by good chance, William Duncan had moved with his Christian converts to establish a new village at Metlakatla, just in time to avoid the arrival of the disease. On Bonilla Island a party of southern Haidas perished while they waited for good weather to cross Hecate Strait. In a few places doctors or priests vaccinated the Indians and checked the disease, but in most areas, as the *Colonist* put it, it raged unchecked until it exhausted itself for want of material to work on. When the epidemic started, there were about 60,000 Indians in British Columbia. When it had burned itself out two or three years later, there were about 40,000.

Smallpox was not the only disease that cut deeply into the Indian population. Epidemics of measles, influenza, tuberculosis and others also took their heavy tolls. Venereal disease, a result of prevalent prostitution, killed many and rendered infertile many more. Alcohol, introduced early as an item of trade, diluted and adulterated in various ways, was also the direct or indirect cause of many deaths.

Few Indians here, in comparison with other parts of the continent, were killed in battles with the white men. Along the coast there were a few small but spectacular massacres of the crews of trading ships, or of Indians attempting to capture them, and several bombardments of villages by naval vessels. In the interior there were very few attacks on trading posts, and one or two armed clashes, much too small to be called Indian wars.*

The Indians' own intertribal wars were quite another matter; the introduction of firearms made these much more lethal affairs, and the mortality rates, especially along the coast, came to be terribly high. It is difficult to gain an appreciation of the destructiveness of this warfare without going over, one by one, the traditional histories of each of the tribes. Murders, massacres to avenge them, and more massacres in retaliation form a constantly recurring pattern. Many small tribes were, in effect, exterminated. Some of the more powerful tribes, or alliances of tribes, embarked on contests of mutual annihilation. The wars continued without abatement into the 1860s. In the early journals we find frequent comments about the constant fighting among the Indians, but these somehow fail to convey the extent of the slaughter that was occurring just beyond the gaze of the men in the trading posts.

FIRST CENSUSES

Detailed and accurate censuses were not made until Indian agents were appointed in the 1880s and 1890s. The agents came to the Indians near the end of their great decline. A few decades earlier they had been large, proud and well-organized societies, far outnumbering the whites, and worthy of respect and even fear. Now, one could almost say, they had become a sick and demoralized minority, to be pitied, converted and administered. In Table 3 the total population in 1885 is given as 28,000, and we should explain why this figure is so much lower than the Indian

---

* Accounts of many of the Indian-white clashes may be found in B.A. McKelvie's little book, *Tales of Conflict* (1949).

Department's own total for that year, which was 38,470. The latter figure included estimates totalling 20,000 for tribes that had not yet been counted. These estimates tended to be carried along without change from year to year, and as it turned out they were much too high; in fact, some of the "bands not visited" did not even exist. For example, the 1890 census shows a long-standing estimate of 2,000 "Heiltsuk" and also an actual count of 300 "Bella Bella", the same tribe! In 1892 the report carried estimates of 2,274 "Hiletsuck", 1,000 "Tahelie" and 8,522 "bands not visited", and gave a total for that year of 34,959. In the 1893 report the non-existent "Hiletsuck" and "Tahelie" were quietly dropped and the estimate for "bands not visited" was revised downward to 2,500, giving a total closer to reality: 25,618.

CHECKING THE DECLINE

For the province as a whole, the decline was effectively checked by about 1890, although the total Indian population continued to decrease very slowly to a low point of 22,605 in 1929. As Table 3 shows, however, the decline was checked at different times in different parts of the province. In the northern interior the numbers have tended to increase, though slowly, ever since the first censuses. In the southern interior recovery also began early, about 1890. It was later in coming to the coast, making itself felt about 1915 in the northern (Tsimshian, Haida, Northern Kwakiutl) and southern (Coast Salish) sections, and not until about 1929 (Kwakiutl) and in 1939 (Nootka) in the central section. These differences reflect the willingness of the different tribes to remould their lives into new patterns and adopt more healthful living conditions.

RAPID INCREASE

Since about 1939, the Indian populations in all parts of the province have been increasing at a faster and faster rate. Their numbers are now back to what they were about 1865, and are more than two-thirds higher than they were in 1929. The number of registered Indians in 1963 was approximately 40,800.

Birth and death rates are computed by the Division of Vital Statistics for "Indians by racial origin" rather than for registered Indians, and, as will be explained later, these are not entirely the same thing. The 1961 figures show this birth rate to be more than 2½ times as high as that of the non-Indian population (59.2 per thousand as compared with 22.8), the death rate to be only slightly higher (11.8 as against 8.8), and the resulting rate of natural increase to be more than three times as high (47.4 as against 14.0). A population with that rate of increase doubles itself in 15 years. This does not mean that the number of registered Indians will double in that time, because part of the increase, though racially Indian, will be legally non-Indian. Neither does it mean that the racial composition of the general population will be greatly altered, because the Indians now make up only 2.3 per cent of the total. The striking contrast between the Indian and non-Indian rates of natural increase may be partially explained by pointing out that the Indian population is a very young population, while the non-Indian population is relatively old. The Indian rate may be expected to level off to some degree when the Indian population attains a more normal age distribution. Be that as it may, the rate still seems to be increasing.

Another measure of how rapidly a population is renewing itself is the "total fertility rate", and by this standard the Indians are twice as fertile as the non-Indians. The Indian rate is 8.029 (which means that Indian women on average have eight children during their reproductive years), while the general rate for British Columbia is 3.944. The reasons usually given for this rapid increase of the Indians – better living conditions, better medical care, lack of birth control and so on – may not provide the whole explanation. It is possible that other factors may be involved; for example, the biological phenomenon of heterosis (hybrid vigour) that results in unusually abundant and fertile progeny when different races interbreed.

THE PRESENT INDIAN POPULATION

Two Kinds of Indians

As a result of intermixture with non-Indians, which has been going on for about five generations, the Indian population, genetically speaking, is becoming less purely "Indian" all the time. Also, more and more people who have some Indian blood are being assimilated into the general population and losing their identity as Indians. Today it is impossible to say how many "Indians" there are without first defining more or less arbitrarily what the word is to mean.

Two different definitions are in official use at the present time, and these do not apply to entirely the same group of people. The first, which refers to what are usually called "registered Indians", is the legal definition used by the Indian Affairs Branch for the people who come under the jurisdiction of the Indian Act, that is, those whose names are included on the official Indian Register, either on a Band List or a General List. (The only "General List Indians" in British Columbia are 17 persons in the New Westminster Agency.) Registered Indians do not necessarily live on Indian reserves; some even live outside the province. Some of them (in-marrying wives) are not of Indian racial origin. Legal status as an Indian is acquired at birth if the father is an Indian, or by marriage to an Indian husband. Illegitimate children of Indian women are also usually granted Indian status. Indian status is given up by "enfranchisement", which is automatic for women marrying non-Indian husbands, and otherwise voluntary, by application. An Indian woman who marries a non-Indian husband thus loses her Indian status, as do in most cases any minor children she may already have, and all children resulting from the marriage. A non-Indian woman who marries an Indian, on the other hand, assumes Indian status, and children of the marriage are also regarded as Indian.

The second definition refers to "Indians by racial origin", and is used by the Dominion Bureau of Statistics and the Division of Vital Statistics. It includes all residents whose racial origin, traced through the father, is Indian. These are not all registered Indians, nor do they all live on Indian reserves.

In 1963 there were about 40,800 registered Indians in British Columbia, according to the Indian Affairs Branch census by agencies and bands.* Of these, about 7,500 were living off reserves. The number of Indians by racial origin is slightly larger: in 1961 the federal census gave a total of 38,814, of whom 30,742 were residing on reserves, while the number of registered Indians in 1961 was 38,261, of whom 32,829 were listed as "on reserve". Neither of these definitions includes all the people who for one reason or another consider themselves to be Indian, or at least identify themselves personally with Indian matters. That number would be considerably higher than the figures given above.

Since the two definitions of "Indian" encompass somewhat different segments of the general population, trends that apply to one do not necessarily apply equally to the other. Such is the case with the rate of increase. Indians by racial origin form a "natural" segment of the population which gains members only by birth and loses them only by death. Registered Indians form an unnatural, legally defined group that gains members by marriage as well as birth, and loses members by marriage and enfranchisement as well as death. The natural increase rate of racial Indians is now a phenomenal 47.4 per thousand, but the growth rate of the legal Indian group is not that fast, because each year it loses more members by marriage and enfranchisement than it gains by marriage. In 1954, the only year for which figures are available (Hawthorn et al. 1958, p. 481), it lost 64 women by marriage and an additional 110 persons (a few large families) by enfranchisement, while gaining only 27 women by marriage, for a net loss of 147. The loss of so many women just entering their child-bearing years also tends to slow the rate of growth of this group. Based on actual performance over the past five years as revealed by the Indian Affairs Branch censuses, the number of

* The figure is inexact because it is difficult to say how many Indians of the Yukon Agency live in British Columbia. I have included all of the Tahltan Band, about 100 Liard River and about 50 Atlin-Teslin.

registered Indians appears to be increasing at a rate of about 30 per thousand (the increase between 1958 and 1959 was 3.15 per cent, and between 1962 and 1963 it was 2.94 per cent*). If that rate continues, the number will double in about 23 years, passing the 80,000 mark by 1985.

The high rate of intermarriage is clearly revealed by the figures for 1954. Of the 248 marriages in British Columbia involving Indians, 91 (37 per cent) were with non-Indians. Of the 221 Indian women who got married, 64 (29 per cent) married non-Indians and assumed "white" status. Of the 184 Indian men who married, 27 (15 per cent) did so with non-Indian women. One notices that 37 fewer Indian men got married than Indian women, and one wonders where they would eventually find wives. Quite possibly the excess of marriageable men over marriageable women is inducing the men to seek eligible brides in the younger age-groups, and this in turn is resulting in earlier marriages for the women.

The process of voluntary enfranchisement permits Indians who are regarded as qualified to relinquish their Indian status and become, for all legal purposes, "white". The status of their wives and minor children changes as well. Upon enfranchisement each individual receives a per capita share of the band fund of his band. He may not return to the reserve to live and cannot regain his Indian status. The developments of recent years have made the process of enfranchisement (and the word) obsolete. All Indians now have the franchise and other rights of citizenship, and there is little incentive for them to relinquish their Indian status. As a method of assimilating Indians into the general population, the process is ineffective. Legal provision by which an entire band may become enfranchised is in existence, but has never been used in British Columbia.

---

* Calculations do not include the Yukon Agency.

A Young Population

As a result of the recent rapid increase, the (registered) Indians of today form an extraordinarily young population. Their median age is between 15 and 16, while that of the non-Indians of the province is about 30. There are exceedingly large numbers of infants and children: 35 per cent of the Indians are under 10, compared with 22 per cent in the general population. There are also large numbers of teenagers; 23 per cent are between 10 and 20, compared with 15 per cent in the general population. Adults of working age are proportionately few: 36 per cent in the 20–60 age bracket, as against 49 per cent in the province as a whole. Elderly Indians are even fewer: only 6 per cent are over 60, as against 13 per cent in the general population. One-quarter of the Indians are 6 or under, half are under 16, three-quarters are under 32.*

Such a lopsided age distribution obviously aggravates the Indians' economic problems. Even if they were the most highly paid wage-earners in the province, the relatively small number of men of working age would be hard pressed to provide housing, clothing and education for the large numbers of children. But they have a relatively low rate of employment, and relatively low incomes. The age-profile is also reflected in medical statistics, especially those showing causes of death. Heart disease and cancer, the main causes of death in the non-Indian population, show only a small incidence among Indians. The principal single cause of death among Indians is accidents – drowning, alcohol, fire, car accidents, poison, falls. One of every five Indian deaths is by accident, a rate four times higher than among the rest of the population. Infant mortality ranks second; although its rate has been cut greatly during the last few years, it is still three times as frequent as among non-Indians. Tuberculosis caused only six deaths in 1960, and is no longer the scourge that it was only a few decades ago. Pneumonia shows a relatively high incidence among Indians, and probably reflects the generally poorer health of these people. The Indians require a disproportionate amount

* Calculated from figures provided by the Indian Affairs Branch as of January 1, 1962.

of hospital care: although their average stay in hospital is about the same as for non-Indians (10.1 days compared with 9.8), they are hospitalized twice as frequently (359.8 cases per thousand, as against 170.8).

A SCATTERED POPULATION

Generally speaking, the Indians live in small settlements scattered throughout the province, much as they did in aboriginal times. They were not driven from their home territories and "placed on reservations", as was the case in other parts of the continent. Instead, the villages and other sites used by each local band were marked off as Indian reserves. The allocation of reserves was all but completed by 1916, and at that time 231 bands were recognized and they had been allotted some 1,900 reserves. This system was a humane one, but it has had the effect of perpetuating the aboriginal pattern of settlement in the face of changing conditions. An Indian is not simply an Indian, he is a member of a specific band whose home is in a specific part of the province. His tie is with his home band, and his band is tied with its own reserves. The effect is to inhibit the mobility of Indian individuals and bands, and to inhibit the formation of larger Indian communities.

It is true that the aboriginal pattern has been modified in its details over the years. During the decades of falling population, many small outlying groups dwindled away, or their remnants converged on the larger centres. A similar process is still going on, as may be seen from the steady decrease in the number of bands, from 231 in 1916 to 191 today. This decrease is not a result of bands becoming extinct (only one, the Arrow Lakes band, has officially gone extinct*), but of amalgamations of small bands into larger ones as the people converge into fewer settlements. More such

---

* Note for the new edition: Descendants of the Arrow Lakes people from the United States approached the Royal British Columbia Museum in 1990 concerning ancestral remains found at the Vallican Site near South Slocan.

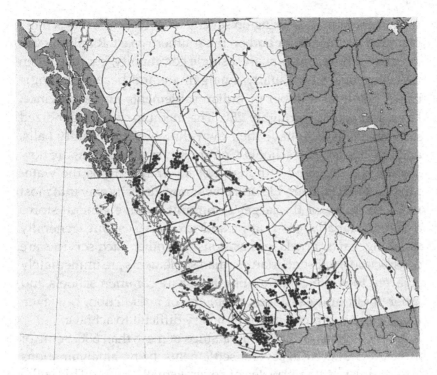

Map 4. Indians of British Columbia: Population Distribution, 1963. Heavy lines show Indian Agencies. One dot represents 100 persons.

amalgamations are being contemplated. But despite these modifications the old pattern remains fundamentally unchanged; indeed, with the population promising to double in the next generation, one might almost say that it is being re-established.

The Indian settlements of today are usually too small to form self-sufficient communities. Only 42 of the 191 bands* have more than 300 members. Of the rest, 81 have between 100 and 300 members, and the remaining 68 have less than 100 (6 bands have less than 10 members). A band may occupy one settlement or it may be scattered in several. In many instances it forms a single community on one of its reserves; this is the usual situation on the northern coast. In other cases it consists of several settlements

---

* This figure includes the Tahltan, Liard River and Atlin-Teslin bands of the Yukon Agency, and excludes the General List group in the New Westminster Agency.

or scattered families living on several of its reserves; this is more common in the interior and on the southern coast. Rarely, if ever, do two or more bands share a single community, because when that happens they usually amalgamate and become a single band. The total number of Indian settlements in the province, large and small, is roughly 250. The medium- and larger-sized settlements usually have their own churches, community halls, and (in 70 cases) day schools. Community water systems are now standard equipment, although not too frequently is the water piped into the houses. Electric power now finds its way into most villages. A few of the larger communities have general stores and, occasionally, gas pumps and taxi services, but, generally speaking, cafes, hotels, gas stations and other such services are conspicuously absent. Many Indian settlements are immediately adjacent to white communities and share common schools and other community services. Problems of jurisdiction, however, make more complete integration very difficult to achieve.

In 1963, 15 bands had memberships of more than 600. Some of these are scattered in several settlements, being amalgamations for administrative purposes of several small groups. This is the case, for example, with the Cowichan band, largest in the province with 1,228 members, but actually an amalgamation of seven smaller bands in the vicinity of Duncan. The Squamish band of Squamish and North Vancouver (955) is similarly an amalgamation of 16 small bands that shared the Squamish language, and is scattered on several reserves. Other large but scattered bands are Lytton (826), Okanagan (774), Mount Currie or Pemberton (768), and Babine (739). The largest Indian "towns" are on the northern part of the coast. Bella Bella leads the list with 949 residents (this is the "on reserve" figure, the total band membership is 970). Masset comes next with 678 (903), followed by Port Simpson with 715 (1,049), Kitimaat with 680 (721) and Alert Bay with 577 (Nimpkish Band, 686).

Of British Columbia's 40,800 Indians, 7,500 are listed as living "off reserve". Many of these have moved permanently to the larger cities and towns without relinquishing their band membership. Others live off the reserve in nearby white communities, or on reserves of other bands, or in the United States.

The old pattern of settlement hangs on from the past, but the old patterns of culture that brought it into existence are gone, or almost gone. There is no reason to suppose that a settlement pattern that evolved over the centuries in a simple fishing and hunting society will serve just as well in the highly centralized and industrialized society into which the Indians must fit today. The directions in which the pattern should change are perhaps shown by the directions in which it has tended to change already: numbers of individuals have moved "off reserve", bands have relocated themselves closer to the main centres of population, small bands have amalgamated to form fewer and larger ones. The administrative framework tends to inhibit these spontaneous changes. Perhaps with slight alterations it could encourage them instead, and help to evolve an Indian settlement pattern more in harmony with the modern social structure of the province.

Alert Bay in the 1950s. A European-style house sits on the site of an ancient big house, whose support posts still stand. Wilson Duff photograph, RBCM PN2078.

The Impact of the White Man

Wherever European civilization has extended its dominance over areas occupied by peoples of less complex culture, the native populations have declined and the native ways of life have disintegrated. British Columbia was no exception to this rule. But the story was not just that simple. The Indian population, as we have seen, did decline from the time of first contact, and dropped to less than a third of its original numbers before beginning its present rapid recovery. But the Indian cultures, especially those of the coastal tribes, were not so much disrupted by the early contacts as they were stimulated to new growth. Any culture can benefit from new introductions if these are of a kind that can be adapted to the existing pattern of life – that is how most human progress occurs. To the native cultures, the new wealth, new materials and new ideas brought by the maritime traders during the early decades of contact proved a potent stimulus. The arts and crafts, trade and technology, social and ceremonial life were all brought to new peaks of development. The climax of Indian culture was reached well after the arrival of the white man on the scene.

But even in the early decades, destructive influences were present – introduced diseases, alcohol, demoralization. To these were later added the disruptive effects of encroachment by white settlers, the imposition of outside laws and suppression of native customs, and the persuasion of missionaries advocating new ways of life. Change came on too strongly, and the Indian cultures ceased to function as effective integrated systems of living. Today the Indian people find themselves in a difficult situation, not entirely of their own making, somewhere between two ways of life, increasing rapidly in numbers and faced with the problem of finding a satisfactory place in the larger society of which they now form a part.

Because the effects of white contact on the Indian cultures have not been uniform over the years, it is best to discuss them in three periods:

    1. The Fur-Trade Period (1774-1849).
    2. The Colonial Period (1849-1871).
    3. The Period Since Confederation.

THE FUR-TRADE PERIOD: STIMULUS TO CULTURE GROWTH

From 1774 to 1849 the white men who ventured to this remote part of the world were here primarily to trade for furs. For most of that time, during the period of the maritime fur trade, they came only as seasonal visitors, seldom so much as stepping ashore. They had little, if any, interest in founding settlements or imposing new ways of life on the Indians. Even after the establishment of the North West Company forts in the interior, beginning with Fort McLeod in 1805*, and the Hudson's Bay Company forts on the coast, beginning with Fort Langley in 1827, the whites were concerned predominantly with their own commerce and safety, and made little effort to influence Indian life. There was no administration and only the beginnings of missionary activity.

The Indians were able to enjoy the economic benefits of the trade without the disruptive effects of colonization. There is no question that the effects on their cultures were profound. There is, however, some debate over just how profound they were. One

---

* Note for the new edition: New information has revealed that two forts were built in the interior before 1805: Rocky Mountain Fort, in 1794, and Rocky Mountain Portage House, in 1804.

well-known authority, Marius Barbeau, believes that much of what is commonly considered to be aboriginal in coastal Indian culture, such as the clan system, the use of crests, and the carving of totem poles, did not exist before the time of contact, but was in a sense a product of the fur trade. Other studies of the same evidence, however, do not support that conclusion (Duff 1964). Another scholar, in an admirable study of the problem, concluded that the fur trade caused no fundamental change in coastal Indian culture, and that the post-contact developments represented only "an expansion and an intensification of prevailing cultural emphases and directions" (Wike 1951, p. 91). In short, the trade stimulated the culture to further growth, but that growth was along its own distinctive lines.

FIRST CONTACTS

Two hundred years ago the northwest coast of North America was one of the least known areas of the world, but exploration was reaching toward it by sea and land. To the northwest, Russian explorers and traders were moving into the Aleutians, and one expedition, that of Bering in 1741, had reached the coast near Cross Sound, where it had lost two boats carrying 15 men. To the south, the Spanish had established settlements in Mexico and California. To the east, British and American fur-traders were working their way across the continent. The first Europeans seen by the Indians of our part of the coast were Spaniards. In 1774 a vessel under the command of Juan Perez was sent from Mexico to explore the coastline and trade with the Indians. It reached the vicinity of the Queen Charlotte Islands, then returned south to Nootka, where it stayed a few days to trade. In 1775 two more Spanish ships came north. One of them reached as far north as the coast of Alaska, where its commander, Juan Francisco Bodega y Quadra, went ashore and took possession of the land for Spain. The next ships to arrive, in 1778, were English, the *Resolution* and the *Discovery* under James Cook.

Captain Cook stayed for a considerable time at Nootka overhauling his ships and trading with the Indians. Among the native

Captain Cook's arrival in Nootka Sound. R.J. Banks illustration. BCARS PDP00494.

goods he received in trade were a number of the soft, luxuriant furs of the Sea Otter, and when his ship later reached China it was found that these furs could be sold for very high prices. As soon as this news was published in Europe, trading ships of several nations flocked to the coast to obtain Sea Otter furs for the China trade.

The rush began in 1785, and during the next quarter century many scores of ships visited the coast. For the first few years the trade was dominated by the English ("King George men" to the Indians), but there was an increasing number of Americans ("Boston men") and a number of Spanish and French as well. After 1800 the number of ships fell off gradually each year, and from that time until the Hudson's Bay Company became active on the coast, the trade was conducted mainly by Yankee ships. Their usual practice was to load their vessels with such trade goods as iron, copper, brass, muskets, cloth, rum and trinkets, sail around Cape Horn and up the northwest coast, trade with the Indians for furs, then take these directly to China and obtain a cargo of tea, spices, silk, ginger and porcelain for the voyage home. While on the coast they made no attempt to annex territories or convert the natives. Their one motive was profit, and after driving as hard a bargain as possible they went about their business, leaving the Indians to do the same.

Quite early, Spain saw the mounting trade as a threat to her Pacific empire, and in 1789 established a settlement at Nootka. But Britain pressed a more vigorous claim, and in 1793 Captain Vancouver accepted possession of the settlement from Commandant Quadra, and it was soon abandoned. Farther up the coast, Russian traders established permanent bases at Kodiak in 1783 and Sitka in 1799. From here they occasionally made forays with Aleut hunters as far south as California.

In the interior, the Indians felt the effects of the white men's presence before they actually saw any. Horses, guns and other trade items passed quickly from tribe to tribe from the south and cast in advance of the first explorers. So did diseases such as smallpox, and some European religious ideas. Stories of strange ships and strange men, and some trade goods, filtered to them from the coast.

It was the adventurous fur-traders of the North West Company who first crossed the Rocky Mountains from the east and reached the coast, and the first of these was Alexander Mackenzie. In 1793 he ascended the Peace River and travelled by way of the Fraser and West Road rivers to the coast at the mouth of the Bella Coola River, the first white man to reach the Pacific overland from Canada. (In that same year Captain Vancouver was exploring the same part of the coast.) Other famous North West Company explorers were Simon Fraser, who in 1808 descended the Fraser River to the sea, and David Thompson, who in 1811 culminated his explorations of the Columbia River by following it to its mouth (where he found Fort Astoria just established). Beginning in 1805 the North West Company founded trading posts in the northern interior, then known as New Caledonia. In 1821 it lost its identity by amalgamating with the Hudson's Bay Company. In 1824 Fort Vancouver, on the Columbia River near its mouth, was established as the headquarters for the coastal trade, and vessels operating from there set up posts along the northwest coast. Fort Langley was the first of these, in 1827. Several others followed: Fort Simpson, established in 1831 on the Nass River and moved to its present location in 1834; Fort McLoughlin (Bella Bella), established in 1833 and abandoned in 1843; Fort Durham (Taku), established in 1840 and abandoned in 1843; Fort Victoria, established in 1843; and Fort Rupert, established in 1849. In 1849, after the Americans had established their claim to the lower Columbia River, the Hudson's Bay Company moved its coastal headquarters to Fort Victoria.

First Impressions

Indian traditions give some idea of what the Indians thought about the first white men they saw, and early journals tell of the white men's first impressions of the Indians. Several things impressed the Europeans very much. They admired the beautiful, seaworthy Indian canoes, some of which were almost as long as their own ships. Although the Indians did not use sails, they were obviously fine seamen, and they very quickly adopted the use of sails (Howay 1941). They already had some iron tools (most likely obtained by way of native trade routes from Asia), so that they were familiar with the metal, and they wanted more. Their workmanship with these tools was excellent: their houses, canoes, totem poles, rattles, boxes and other implements all drew favourable comment in the early journals. To those who visited their homes, the Indians showed generous and dignified hospitality, greeting them with food, speeches and songs. Captain Cook noted especially the "bashfulness and modesty" of the women, and the Indians' disgust on first tasting liquor (see also Howay 1942).

The Indians at first did not know what to think of the bearded, light-skinned strangers. Some, for a while, thought they were supernatural creatures like those known from ancient traditions. Near Yale the Indians told Simon Fraser that someone like him had once come up the river and left scratch-marks on the rocks, a local story that refers to the mythical Transformer Haylse. The newcomers were strange in many ways. For one thing, they were all males. They owned many wonderful things – "magic sticks" (as the Kwakiutl called muskets), clocks, uniforms with buttons and buckles. Telescopes seemed magical, too: one Haida chief asked Captain Ingraham to look around a point of land to see if enemies were approaching. The Haida called white men *Yets-haida* ("iron men") because they were so rich in that valued metal; the Nootka called them *Mamathni* ("their houses move over the water").

But once the novelty wore off, the Indians gave further thought to dealing with these new men. They were not relatives, so perhaps should be treated like members of distant tribes, as potential enemies. Then it would be fair to steal from them or even kill them if there was an advantage to be gained. Some of the white traders, for their part, used unfair methods with the Indians and were touchy and suspicious, ready to use their guns to put the natives in their place. Inevitably, clashes occurred, and several bloody fights dot the history of the maritime fur-trade period.

The Nature of the Trade

It is important to understand how intense the trade quickly became.* Within a very few years after 1785 the entire coast was glutted with trade goods. The Indians were by no means passive recipients of whatever trinkets the traders chose to offer; they held out for goods they wanted and drove hard bargains. In the earliest years the item they most wanted was iron in the form of chisels, but after a few years many tribes began to reject the metal, or demanded that it be forged into such forms as fancy collars and bracelets. Copper was also in strong demand at first, its value being set by the small amounts of native copper already present, and highly prized, when the white men came. But by 1800 the coast was saturated with copper, and the demand fell off. Muskets and ammunition were in general use on the coast by about 1794, and remained in steady demand. Blankets and cloth were also in constant demand and were to become the standards

---

* This section follows ideas expressed in Wike 1951.

of value in the trade. European clothing was a popular trade item, and some chiefs soon sported wonderful ensembles of uniforms and ornaments. The demand for beads and trinkets suffered from the whims of fashion; blue glass beads were the most consistently popular, but the traders found it impossible to predict what the Indians' preferences would be. Alcohol, after the Indians had conquered their initial revulsion to it, became popular and remained in constant demand. As profitable side-lines the traders soon learned to add to their stock certain prod-ucts of the country; for example, elk hides from the Columbia River were in demand on the coast for use as armour, and the brilliant abalone shell of Mexico and California was much pre-ferred for ornamentation by the northern tribes over the pallid local variety.

After the first decade or so the staple items of trade had be-come blankets, muskets, powder, shot, cloth, molasses, rice, bread and biscuits. Secondary items used as presents included tobacco, beads, buttons, brass wire, chisels, needles, thread, knives, scissors, stockings and apples (Wike 1951, p. 53).

CHANGES IN NATIVE LIFE

The fur trade produced no major revolution in coastal Indian life, compared, for example, to the effects of the horse and the gun on Plains Indian life. But it brought prosperity, an increase in wealth in a society already organized around wealth. The new tools and guns increased the Indians' productive efficiency, and the outlet of the European market for furs brought them increased returns. The new wealth strengthened the existing social and economic systems rather than weakening them. The chiefs, who controlled Sea Otter hunting and trade relations, became richer and more secure. More wealth meant more and bigger potlatches and a more active ceremonial life, with more need for artistic products. In the words of Wike (1951, p. 102), "Northwest Coast society rushed out to meet the Sea Otter trade, to use it, and to shape it to the society's own ends."

Native Trade

The first chiefs to contact the traders were able to turn the white man's desire for furs to their own advantage. To the furs they obtained by hunting they could add large numbers obtained by an easier method: trade with other tribes not yet visited by whites. This required only an expansion of existing trade patterns. Some of the Nootka and Haida chiefs very early tried to claim monopolies and act as middlemen between the traders and the other tribes. Later, in the 1830s, Kwakiutl traders travelled along the coast, buying furs at higher prices than the Hudson's Bay Company was paying, and selling them to Yankee ships. More remarkable still were the Tsimshian and Tlingit chiefs who took control over all the trade along the Skeena and Stikine rivers. So profitable was their business that they fought the white traders to keep them away. One Tlingit chief even led a war party inland and wiped out a small Hudson's Bay post that threatened his trade monopoly.

The increased commerce between the coastal and interior tribes produced other effects. Through trade relations and intermarriage, interior tribes such as the Carrier and Tahltan began to adopt the social systems and ceremonies of their more powerful coastal neighbours, a process that has continued almost to the present. Farther north, around Atlin and Teslin lakes, the original Athapaskan people were so thoroughly altered in culture and language that they are now regarded as Inland Tlingit.

Another result of the fur trade was the clustering of Indian tribes about the forts, for trade advantages and protection, or just out of curiosity. This produced larger concentrations of population than had ever gathered in one place before. For example, nine tribes of Tsimshian moved to Fort Simpson (Port Simpson) soon after its establishment in 1834, and four tribes of Kwakiutl converged on Fort Rupert soon after 1849. These larger groupings raised new questions on how the tribes and families were to be ranked, and set the stage for greater potlatches and winter ceremonies than ever before.

Potlatching

A potlatch was a large gathering to which important people were invited in order to witness some event, such as a young person assuming a new name or the completion of a new house and erection of a totem pole. On such an occasion the host would display his wealth and present gifts to his guests. The more he gave away, the more prestige he acquired. Every person wanted to raise himself in rank, and most had some claim through inheritance to more important positions, but it was only by means of potlatching that one could assume and hold the positions of high rank. After the time of contact, potlatches became more numerous and larger. More wealth was available, and the higher death rate resulted in more positions of importance being open. The competition to fill them was keen.

Potlatching also changed in character. Among the Kwakiutl at least, it became a substitute for war. Before the imposition of

A potlatch at Alert Bay in the early 20th century, showing gifts to be distributed: frontlets, bowls, bracelets, etc. William Halliday photograph, RBCM PN10628.

British law, war had been a major method of humbling enemy tribes and gaining prestige. During the 1850s and 1860s warfare decreased and potlatching increased. Energies formerly expended in war were now put into potlatches, which were organized like war campaigns and referred to in the speeches as wars. One old Kwakiutl said in a speech in 1895: "When I was young I saw streams of blood shed in war. But since that time the white men came and stopped up that stream of blood with wealth. Now we fight with our wealth."

Art

The fur-trade years were also great ones for the native artists; Northwest Coast art reached its highest peaks several decades after the white men came. This distinctive art style was already in existence at the time of contact (the role of the pre-contact iron tools in developing the style is still not fully understood). But for their more-frequent feasts and ceremonies the chiefs needed more carved headdresses, masks, costumes, staffs, feast dishes, spoons and many other things, and they kept the artists busy producing them. New tools permitted the artists to work with greater ease and refinement. The white traders were not blind to the quality of the art that was being produced, and soon the demand for curios grew to large proportions. It was in this way that the famous Haida argillite carving originated and thrived. Totem poles enjoyed an especially great elaboration during those years. Carved house posts, house frontal poles, mortuary and memorial poles had all been in use before the time of contact. But with the new wealth and new tools, more totem poles were erected and the types became larger and more elaborate. The forests of carved columns that stood in up-coast villages several decades ago were the products of this golden age of Indian art.

Guns

Noisy and short-ranged, the first muskets obtained by the Indians did not wholly replace the bow and harpoon for hunting purposes. But they did to a great extent replace the club and dagger for purposes of war. Warfare suddenly became much more deadly. On the coast some villages were practically wiped out, and in at least one instance a warlike tribe decimated its neighbours and moved into their territories. This happened in the vicinity of Cape Mudge and Campbell River. When Vancouver passed this way in 1792 on his survey of the coast, he found the area occupied by Salish-speaking people who had no guns. Farther north on Vancouver Island, at "Cheslakee's Village" at the mouth of the Nimpkish River, he noticed that the Kwakiutl chief had eight muskets, obtained from the Nootka. Soon after that date the Kwakiutl raided and terrorized the Salish tribes along the Strait of Georgia and Puget Sound. In the extensive warfare that followed, both sides suffered very heavy losses, but the end result was that the Southern Kwakiutl displaced the decimated Comox Indians of Cape Mudge and Campbell River.

In the interior, too, the arrival of guns (and also horses) stimulated warfare and caused reshuffling of tribal territories. The Kootenay, for example, formerly held territories in the plains east of the Rockies. Their Blackfoot enemies acquired guns and horses first, and for self-defence they retired through the mountains and made their homes along the Kootenay River, returning to the plains only seasonally to hunt Bison. Farther north also, other tribes were pushed west across the Rockies. The Sekani and Beaver both formerly lived in Alberta, but about 1784 the Beaver obtained muskets and forced the Sekani up the Peace River into the interior of British Columbia. Then the Sekani in their turn acquired guns and were dominant for a time, taking over large territories as far west as Bear Lake.

THE COLONIAL PERIOD:
FORMATIVE YEARS

For a short time Vancouver Island and British Columbia were British colonies quite separate from Canada, and this circumstance has left its mark on Indian policies even to the present day. In 1849 the imperial government saw the necessity of colonizing Vancouver Island in order to confirm British sovereignty in the area. The government entrusted the task to the Hudson's Bay Company, a competent British organization already well established in the country, temporarily granting title of the land of Vancouver Island to the Company. It also sent out from England the first Governor, Richard Blanshard, but he soon resigned, and James Douglas, Chief Factor of the Company, was named Governor in 1851. When the mainland colony of British Columbia was brought into existence in 1858, Douglas gave up his position in the Company and became its Governor as well, and he served

James Douglas. Fardon photograph, BCARS A01232.

both colonies until his retirement in 1864. In 1866 the two colonies were united into one, which entered Confederation as the Province of British Columbia in 1871.

It was during these two important decades that the basic features of Indian administration were established. Before this time it had been Company policy to treat the Indians as fairly as possible and interfere with them only when they molested a white man. The arrival of colonists intent on taking up land raised a whole new set of problems. Some agreement had to be reached on the ownership of land, and ways had to be found to make the Indians conform to the laws of the colony. The Indian policies that did evolve were different in important respects from those of Canada, and after Confederation the two sets of policies came into conflict. The long and vexatious resolution of these differences, perhaps not yet completed, has complicated the relationships between the Indians and the governments ever since.

BEGINNINGS OF INDIAN ADMINISTRATIONS

The first policies for administering Indian affairs in this area were formulated by James Douglas. As Chief Factor of the Hudson's Bay Company (until 1858), Governor of Vancouver Island (1851-1864), and Governor of the mainland colony of British Columbia (1858-1864), he settled Indian problems with a firm hand. The imperial government in London provided him with only the broadest statements of policy, and little in the way of specific advice. As colonization progressed, his main concerns, in addition to maintaining law and order, were to purchase the Indian ownership rights to the land and to set aside adequate reserves for their use. Douglas took the usual British view that although the absolute title to the land was vested in the Crown, the Indians did own some proprietary rights to it that should be extinguished by making treaties and paying compensation. Between 1850 and 1854, acting as the agent of the Hudson's Bay Company (since the Company still held title to the land), he made 14 treaties with the tribes living around Victoria, Nanaimo and Fort Rupert. The land was to become "the entire property of the white people forever". The Indians' village sites and enclosed fields were to be reserved for their use (but the Crown retained absolute title to these reserves). Each family was paid compensation amounting to about 2 pounds 10 shillings, and it was understood that the Indians were to retain their right to hunt over unoccupied lands and to carry on their fisheries as formerly.[*]

By 1860, settlement was spreading into the Cowichan, Chemainus and Saltspring Island areas. Governor Douglas made determined efforts to continue the policy of buying out the Indian rights to the land. The local Assembly agreed that it was necessary, and petitioned the imperial government for the necessary funds. The Colonial Secretary also agreed that the step was an absolute necessity, but maintained that the funds should be raised locally. With no funds, Douglas was not able to make treaties, and after his retirement his successors chose to ignore the problem or deny the existence of any Indian title. Despite growing discontent among the Indians, the colonial governments made no further treaties with them.

On the question of Indian reserves, Douglas believed that all cause for discontent would be removed if he gave the Indians as much land as they requested. By the time of his retirement he had set aside a large number of reserves on Vancouver Island and along the Fraser River. His policy was to give the Indians whatever plots of land they chose and as much acreage as they requested (not being farmers they did not ask for very much, in no case more than 10 acres per family). He made no point of moving them away from white settlements, believing that close contact between the races would help to advance the Indians in civilization. His successors considered that his reserve policy had been too open-handed with the limited agricultural land of the colony; they were less generous in establishing new reserves and cut back some of the old ones.[†]

---

[*] Texts of the treaties may be found in Papers Connected with the Indian Land Question, 1850-75 (British Columbia 1875).

[†] The principal sources of the information in this section are Douglas 1874, Shankel 1945 and Cail 1956.

THE PERIOD SINCE CONFEDERATION: YEARS OF CHANGE

When British Columbia became a province of Canada in 1871, the administration of Indian affairs began to undergo profound changes. Jurisdiction passed from the local governor to the distant office of the Secretary of State in Ottawa, where knowledge of the west-coast Indians and their special problems was, to say the least, somewhat limited. Article 13 of the Terms of Union, which dealt with Indian affairs, provided that "the charge of the Indians and the trusteeship and management of the lands reserved for their use and benefit" were to be assumed by the Dominion. From time to time as required, the province was to convey tracts of land to the Dominion in trust for the Indians. The Dominion agreed to continue a policy "as liberal as that hitherto pursued by the British Columbia government". The transition was to prove less than smooth, with the governments disagreeing on the interpretation of these terms and the Indians finding more and more effective ways of presenting their demands themselves. Several years were required to create an administrative structure to handle Indian matters, and several decades to settle the complicated and troublesome problem of Indian reserves. The question of Indian title (the Land Question) was in issue the entire time, and is perhaps still not finally settled. Recent years have seen many new and enlightened advances in the administration of Indian affairs, and the over-all policy of the Indian Affairs Branch is to "work itself out of a job" by finding ways to integrate the Indians as full citizens of their provincial and local communities.

At the beginning of the period the Indians were declining in numbers, and it was fully expected that they would pass out of the picture as a distinct element of the population within a couple of generations. As we have seen, such assimilation did not occur, and they are now rapidly increasing. Most of their languages are still spoken and in little immediate danger of being forgotten. But their ways of life have undergone profound changes, and are still in an unsettled state of rapid change. The old arts and technology have fallen into disuse, except for vestiges that have been preserved and developed as arts and crafts for sale. The Indians have had to enter the white man's economy, and have been confronted with new kinds of employment or new kinds of organization in old employments. Under the frontal attack of missionaries or the law, or just rendered obsolete by changing times, the old forms of social and ceremonial life have all but disappeared. The old religious beliefs and rituals (with a few interesting exceptions) yielded quickly to Christianity, and now the Indians are all nominally Catholic, Anglican, United Church, Salvation Army, Pentecostal or members of the Indian Shaker Church. New problems have induced them to adopt or create new forms of political organization, both on the local band level and on the intertribal level. A sense of Indian identity is growing stronger, and cultural forms that may be called neo-Indian (based partly on old Indian culture but also filling real needs in today's world) are appearing and in some cases thriving. The story is not over yet, but certainly for the foreseeable future at least, the Indians are not going to be assimilated, but will remain as a distinct element of our population and our culture.

Indian Commissioner I.W. Powell (seated centre with heavy black beard) visiting the Kwakiutl at Tsawatti in 1873. Richard Maynard photograph, RBCM PN2291B.

DEVELOPMENT OF INDIAN ADMINISTRATION

In Ottawa at the time of Confederation, Indian Affairs was the responsibility of the Secretary of State. In 1873 it became a branch of the Department of the Interior; in 1880 it was made a separate Department of Indian Affairs; in 1936 it became a branch of the Department of Mines and Resources; and since 1950 it has been the Indian Affairs Branch of the Department of Citizenship and Immigration.

British Columbia is the only province with a Commissioner for Indian Affairs, and has had one from the beginning. Dr I.W. Powell was named as the first Commissioner in 1872. Three years later the province was divided into two sections: a Victoria Superintendency (Vancouver Island and the Northwest Coast) under the charge of Commissioner Powell, and a Fraser River Superintendency or Mainland Division at New Westminster under the charge of James Lenihan. Powell made inspections up the coast in naval vessels in 1873 (HMS *Boxer*), 1879 (HMS *Rocket*) and 1881 (HMS *Rocket*); Lenihan was unable to spend much time in the field because of Indian unrest over the Land Question. In 1880 the two superintendencies were abolished in preparation for the appointment of Indian agents. Powell remained as Commissioner until 1890, when he was replaced by A.W. Vowell.*

In 1881 six agencies were established (Cowichan, West Coast, Kwawkewlth, Fraser River, Kamloops and Okanagan). In 1883 two more were added: Lillooet and Northwest Coast (however, the Indians refused to accept the agent appointed to the latter and it remained inactive until 1888). Since that time several new agencies have been established and several of the old ones subdivided; there are now 20 agencies under the control of the Commissioner, including the Yukon Agency, which takes in the northern part of British Columbia (see Table 4 and Map 5).

---

* Annual reports of the Commissioner and reports from each of the agents after they were appointed were published from 1872 to 1916 (Canada 1872-79 and Canada 1880-1916), and are excellent sources of information. Powell took the photographers Maynard, Hastings and Dossetter respectively on the three trips mentioned, and an excellent photographic record was obtained.

Table 4: Indian Agencies of British Columbia*

Agency	Location	Tribes	Population
Babine	Hazelton	Gitksan, Bulkley River Carrier	2,601
Bella Coola	Bella Coola	Bella Coola, Northern Kwakiutl of Bella Bella and Rivers Inlet, Tsimshian of Kitasoo	1,863
Burns Lake	Burns Lake	Carrier (mostly Babines)	995
Cowichan	Duncan	Coast Salish of Vancouver Island, Pachenat Nootka	3,839
Fort St John	Fort St John	Beaver, Slave, some Cree	683
Kamloops	Kamloops	Shuswap	1,846
Kootenay	Cranbrook	Kootenay, Kinbasket Shuswap	554
Kwawkewlth	Alert Bay	Southern Kwakiutl, Comox	2,560
Lytton	Lytton	Thompson, Lillooet, Shuswap	2,364
New Westminster[1]	New Westminster	Stalo (Coast Salish), Lillooet of Lillooet River	2,585
Nicola	Merritt	Thompson and Okanagan of Upper Nicola	1,235
Okanagan	Vernon	Okanagan and Shuswap of Spallumcheen	1,713
Queen Charlotte	Masset	Haida	1,224
Skeena River	Prince Rupert	Tsimshian, including Kincolith Niska	2,808
Stuart Lake	Vanderhoof[2]	Carrier, Sekani	2,187
Terrace	Terrace	Niska, canyon Tsimshian, Haisla	2,196
Vancouver	Vancouver	Coast Salish of mainland, Lillooet (Interior Salish)	3,328
West Coast	Port Alberni	Nootka	2,788
Williams Lake	Williams Lake	Chilcotin, Carrier, Shuswap	2,634
Yukon (B.C. region)	Whitehorse	Inland Tlingit, Tahltan, Kaska	800
		Total Population:	40,800

---

*   As of December 31 1963.
1   Vancouver and New Westminster Agencies combined in 1964 into a single agency known as the Fraser Agency and based at Vancouver.
2   Stuart Lake Agency office moved to Prince George in 1964.

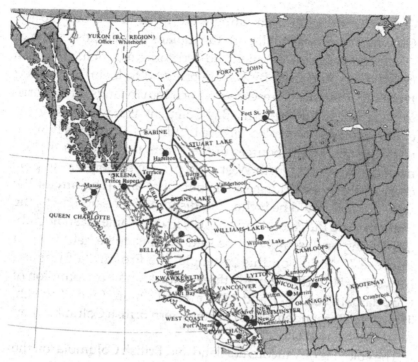

Map 5. Indian Agencies and Agency Offices, 1963.

Indian Reserves and Indian Title

The Indian policies of British Columbia differed from those of the rest of Canada most sharply on matters involving land. First there was the question of recognizing and extinguishing the aboriginal possessory rights or "Indian title". In North America it had been the usual practice, started by Britain and continued by Canada and the United States, to make treaties with the Indian tribes as the country was opened up for settlement. In return for their ownership rights, the Indians received tracts of land for Indian reservations and compensation in the form of money and gifts, services, and perpetual annual payments. The practice was given Royal sanction in 1763, when King George III issued a Proclamation (which had the force of a statute in the colonies) saying in effect that the Indians were not to be dispossessed of their lands without their own consent as well as that of the

Crown, and that Indian lands were to be ceded only to the Crown. No one was to disturb the Indians in their possession of "such Parts of Our Dominion and Territories as, not having been ceded to or purchased by Us, are reserved to them . . . as their Hunting Grounds." It reserved as such Indian lands all the territory granted to the Hudson's Bay Company that was outside the existing colonies, and also "all the Lands and Territories lying to the Westward of the Sources of the Rivers that fall into the Sea from the West and North West." No private person was to purchase any of these Indian lands, but "if at any Time any of the said Indians should be inclined to dispose of the said Lands, the same shall be Purchased only for Us, in our Name, at some public Meeting or Assembly of the said Indians, to be held for that Purpose."* Acting on this principle, the Province of Canada between 1850 and 1862 made three treaties, and the Dominion of Canada between 1871 and 1923 made 12 more (one of which, Treaty No. 8, included part of northeastern British Columbia, and will be discussed later).†

The colonies of Vancouver Island and British Columbia, on the other hand, despite the intentions of all concerned in the beginning, evolved a policy that ignored or denied the existence of any Indian title and therefore any need to make treaties. This oversight has probably not resulted in any relative hardship on the

---

* It is important not to confuse Indian title with the absolute or underlying title to the land. Absolute title (a European concept) has been vested in the Crown ever since Britain, Spain, Russia and the United States, without consulting any Indians, settled the questions of sovereignty over this continent. The Indians of Canada, whether by choice or not and whether they have treaties or not, are subjects of the Crown, and the Crown owns the land. Of course the Indians did own the land previously, under clearly defined concepts of ownership. This "Indian title" has been recognized by the Crown as a burden on its sovereignty, and steps have been taken to extinguish the native rights by treaty. In fact it could be said that by the Royal Proclamation and subsequent precedents the Crown has legally obligated itself to recognize and extinguish Indian title.

† The provisions of these treaties are outlined in *The Canadian Indian* (Canada 1959) and the "Handbook of the Indians of Canada" (Canada 1913).

Indians of the province, but it has kept the Land Question in the category of unfinished business, providing a focus for their sense of grievance and a rallying point for the native spokesmen and intertribal organizations that have appeared to present the Indians' case.

The second problem, closely related, was that of Indian reserves: how much land were the Indians to be given for their own use, and how was it to be safeguarded? Elsewhere in Canada it was the policy to allot each tribe a single large tract of land (either 160 acres or 1 square mile per family), on which they were expected to settle and establish farms. British Columbia's system was better suited to the coastal Indian way of life: each local band was allotted several small reserves that it used intermittently in the course of its migratory activities. In terms of total acreage, however, these compared poorly with the Canadian standard. On entering Confederation, how much land was the province to convey to the Dominion for new reserves? Ottawa maintained that at least 80 acres per family of five was required. The province replied that the coastal tribes would not use that much land, and set a maximum of 20 acres per family for future reserves (and double that amount in the agricultural areas east of the Cascade Mountains). The province also insisted on its "reversionary interest" in reserve lands: if at any time land was cut off a reserve, or a band gave up reserve land, its ownership was to revert to the province.

While the two governments argued, the Indians became more and more agitated. By 1877 the situation in the interior was so tense that an Indian war seemed imminent. In Ottawa the Minister of the Interior thought the situation serious enough to warn the provincial authorities by telegram that his government would side with the Indians in any trouble: "Indian rights to soil in British Columbia have never been extinguished. Should any difficulty occur, steps will be taken to maintain the Indian claims to all the country where rights have not been extinguished by treaty. Don't desire to raise the question at present but local government must instruct Commissioners to make reserves so large as to completely satisfy Indians." He enlarged on these views by letter (Mills 1877). Like James Douglas, he hoped that the vexing question of title could be circumvented by a generous policy of allotting reserves. The commissioners to which he referred were the three members of a Joint Committee on Indian Reserves appointed in 1876. They were empowered to lay out reserves, using no fixed basis of acreage, and subject to the reversionary interest of the province. The Commission was active for more than 30 years. In 1877, however, it was reduced to a single member, Gilbert Malcolm Sproat. Sproat resigned in 1880 and was replaced by Peter O'Reilly, who served until his retirement in 1898. Commissioner Vowell then added this to his other duties, and served until 1908, when all reserve allotments were halted by provincial protests. It was during these three decades that most of the reserves in the province were laid out.*

The province now asked for an adjustment downward in the size of existing reserves. Also, the reversionary interest clause, by which the province immediately became the owner of any land surrendered by the Indians, was causing difficulties of administration. It meant, for example, that the Dominion was not able to sell reserve land for the benefit of the Indians involved, because the land could not be sold until surrendered, and once surrendered it was the property of the province. In 1912 a special Dominion Commissioner, J.A.J. McKenna, was appointed and met with Premier Richard McBride to settle these problems. The result was the McKenna-McBride Agreement. A five-man Royal Commission was to be appointed to make the final and complete allotment of Indian lands in the province. Upon settlement of the number and size of reserves, title was to be conveyed to the Dominion free of any reversionary interest, except in the case of lands belonging to bands that might become extinct. This Royal Commission on Indian Affairs, now usually referred to as the Reserve Commission, was named in 1913, and laboured for three busy years, travelling to all parts of the province and interview-

---

* Annual reports were published by the Reserve Commission, and may be found with the reports of the Superintendent General of Indian Affairs. New edition note: References to documents pertaining to the various reserve commissions and superintendents can be found in Young 1992 and Kennedy 1994.

The Reserve Commission in session in Victoria. RBCM PN12326.

ing virtually all bands. Some of the northern coastal people
refused to discuss their reserve requirements until the question
of Indian title had been settled, and their needs had to be judged
from information given by the Indian agents. In most cases the
Commission confirmed the existing reserves, but it also added
about 87,000 acres of new reserve land and cut off some 47,000
acres of old. Its report, in four volumes, was published in 1916,
and was ratified by both governments in 1924. The reserve lands
were formally conveyed to the Dominion by Order in Council
No. 1036 in 1938. With some minor adjustments since then, this
was the final settlement of Indian Land Question between the
two governments. In 1963 British Columbia's 189 bands owned
a total of 1,620 reserves (of 2,241 in the whole of Canada) with a
total area of 843,479 acres.

To return to the question of Indian title, it was the Nass River
Indians, encouraged at first by missionaries, who took the lead
in agitating for a proper hearing of the Indian case. In 1887 a
three-man Joint Commission was sent up the coast to inquire into
the causes of their unrest. The Nass chiefs presented their case
with eloquence and dignity, but were met by statements of legal

technicalities that they could not comprehend. Again and again they explained that they owned all the land and had never given it up, and they objected to being given a few small reserves. How was it that the land no longer belonged to them, but to the Queen?

>   What we don't like about the government is their saying this: 'We will give you this much land.' How can they give it when it is our own? We cannot understand it. They have never bought it from us or our forefathers. They have never fought and conquered our people and taken the land that way, and yet they say now that they will give us so much land – our own land.

The chiefs asked for a treaty recognizing their aboriginal title, for large reserves, and compensation for the land outside the reserves. The Commission had no power to grant any of these; it had only come to get the facts and make recommendations (British Columbia 1888).

The Indians began to realize that they had to organize and learn new ways of presenting their case. In 1906 a delegation representing the Squamish and other southern coast tribes went to London; they received a hearing but no real satisfaction. The Nass Indians formed the Nishga Land Committee to raise funds and obtain professional legal advice. In 1913 they adopted and sent to Ottawa the Nishga Petition stating their land claim, and asked that it be tested before the highest court, the Judicial Committee of the Privy Council in London. But that body can hear only cases appealed from lower courts; the Indians refused to have their case tried first in a lower (Canadian) court, maintaining truthfully that they had been promised a direct hearing before the Privy Council. Nishga delegations travelled to Ottawa in 1915 and 1916 in unsuccessful attempts to win this concession. In 1916 the Nishga joined with the Interior Salish and southern coast tribes to form the Allied Tribes of British Columbia, a powerful intertribal organization led by the two outstanding Indian leaders of their generation, Peter Kelly and Andrew Paull. Meetings were held, funds raised, and petitions sent to Ottawa. Rejection by the Allied Tribes of the 1916 report of the Reserve

Commission delayed its ratification by the governments until 1924. In 1923 they presented Ottawa with a set of demands in return for which they would drop the issue of Indian title. These included a cash settlement of about 2.5 million dollars, an increase in the size of reserves to 160 acres per person, certain hunting and fishing rights, and extensive educational and medical benefits. The Dominion government thought these demands beyond reason, and delayed no longer in ratifying the Reserve Commission report (as the provincial government had done a short time before).

The Allied Tribes continued to press for a hearing before the Privy Council. In 1926 the government appointed a Special Joint Committee of the Senate and House of Commons to examine their claims. This was a major climax in the history of the Indian title question. The Joint Committee met in haste near the end of the parliamentary session. Although Peter Kelly and Andrew Paull were well received and made a good impression on the members, their legal counsel succeeded in nothing more than antagonizing and infuriating them. The Committee's report has been called The Great Settlement of 1927. It found that the Indians "have not established any claim to the lands of British Columbia based on aboriginal or other title", and decreed that the question of Indian title should now be regarded as closed. Although, they said, the treatment of the Indians of British Columbia was at least as generous as that received by treaty Indians, they recommended that a grant in lieu of treaty payments amounting to $100,000 a year be expended for their benefit, over and above the normal costs of administration.*

The Allied Tribes was a spent force and disbanded. The title question was dropped. Yet it was not forgotten and did not die. With the appearance in recent years of the native brotherhoods and the rebirth of the Nishga Tribal Council, it has to an increasing extent formed a rallying point for a growing Indian nationalism.

---

* "Report and evidence. Special Joint Committee on Claims of the Allied Indian Tribes" (Canada 1927). The report did not say that the Indians did not *have* a claim based on Indian title, only that they had *not established* such a claim.

The Indian side of the Land Question now has able spokesmen in both federal Parliament and the provincial Legislature. Its leaders have been stimulated by the example of the United States in settling its Indian grievances in recent years, and especially by the decision in favour of the Tlingit and Haida of Alaska in the United States Court of Claims (1959), which found the Indians entitled to compensation for their Indian title. In 1961, in Ottawa, another Joint Committee of the Senate and House of Commons on Indian Affairs recommended the establishment of an Indian Claims Commission to settle all outstanding grievances, including specifically the British Columbia Land Question. This commission has been promised by the present government.*

Treaty No. 8

The generalization, often heard, that the Indians of British Columbia are non-treaty Indians is not wholly true. We have already mentioned the treaties made between the Hudson's Bay Company and some of the tribes on Vancouver Island in the early 1850s. In addition, the Beavers and Slaves of the present Fort St John Agency were included in one of the Canadian treaties about the turn of the century, and receive annual treaty payments like most other Canadian Indians. As this was the only instance since Confederation in which Indian title to land within the province was extinguished, it is of considerable historical interest.

As settlement spread westward and northward in Canada, it was the practice of the government to extinguish the Indian rights to the soil by treaty. Treaty No. 8, made in 1899, covered what is now northern Alberta and part of the Northwest Territories, and also included the northeastern corner of British Columbia. Strangely, it seems to have been made without consultation with the provincial government, although title to the land had been vested in the province all along. Also there was, and still remains, some uncertainty as to how much land within the

* More detailed accounts of material in this section may be found in Shankel 1945, Cail 1956, Drucker 1958 and La Violette 1961.

province was covered. By the wording of the treaty, the area concerned was that portion of British Columbia "east of the central
range of the Rocky Mountains" (Canada 1899, p. xlii). But on the
map published in the following year's report to show the territory ceded, a much larger area than that is shown, extending
west all the way to the Pacific divide and including the entire
Peace and Liard drainages. A more recent map in the "Handbook
of Indians of Canada" (Canada 1913) shows a more modest area,
similar to that of the present Fort St John Agency, but even this is
somewhat larger than the area actually occupied by the Indians
involved. A still more recent map of "Indian Treaties" published
by the federal government in 1959 shows the same large area as
on the 1900 map, which includes the territories of the (non-
treaty) Kaska and Sekani.

By the terms of the treaty, the Indians were to give up "all
rights, titles and privileges whatsoever" to the land, and were to
receive in return reserves on a scale of one square mile (259
hectares) per family of five or 160 acres (65 hectares) in severalty;
presents of $32 for chiefs, $22 for headmen and $12 per person,
as well as farming equipment or ammunition, medals and flags;
hunting and fishing rights subject to government regulations;
school teachers; and annual treaty payments of $25 for chiefs, $15
for headmen and $5 per person.

There was some delay in bringing the British Columbia bands
under the treaty. The intention was to include all those who
traded at Fort St John and Fort Nelson. None were actually con-
tacted in 1899, but in 1900 at Fort St John, 46 Beavers accepted
treaty payments. The number rose slowly each year until 1914,
when there were 162. In that same year the Hudson Hope band
of Beavers, numbering 116, was also brought under the treaty, as
were 34 Salteaux (Cree) who had settled a short time before at
Moberly Lake. These three bands were allotted their full entitlement of reserve lands at that time, from land in the Peace River
Block that was then controlled by the Dominion (Canada 1900,
p. xxxix; 1914, pp. 52, 84; 1915, p. 86). The Fort Nelson Indians
were first brought under the treaty in 1910 when 126 Indians,
"mostly Slaves with a few Sicanees", accepted treaty payments.
In the following year, payments were accepted by 131 Slaves and

98 Sekani (Canada 1911, p. 191; 1912, p. 191). Soon after that time almost all the Sekani moved away (to appear as the "Nelson River nomads" in the reports of the Stikine Agency of Telegraph Creek). The Slaves continued to receive treaty payments, but no provision was made to give them Indian reserves. In 1916 the Reserve Commission acknowledged its responsibility to ensure that they should receive the reserves to which the treaty entitled them, but were not able to visit the band. It passed a resolution saying that when the Indian Department found itself able to make a census and recommend suitable lands, these should be conveyed to Canada by the province.* The Slave band did not claim its reserve entitlement until 1956, at which time its extent was set at 24,448 acres. Reserve lands to this amount were transferred to the Dominion in 1961 (Order in Council 2995) as the full and final settlement of Indian lands in the area covered by Treaty No. 8.

Indian Administration Today

The Indians today remain legally different from other Canadians in that they are subject to special legislation (the Indian Act), their public affairs are administered by a special branch of the government (the Indian Affairs Branch) and they possess, though do not fully control, lands of a special legal category (Indian reserves). They differ from other British Columbians in that they look to the federal government, rather than to provincial or municipal governments, for education, health and welfare services, and the direction of much of the everyday business of their lives. The trend of policy is toward the removal of these differences.

Indians now enjoy the same voting rights as other citizens, having gained the provincial franchise in 1949 and the unrestricted federal franchise in 1960 (their first opportunity to use it

---

* Report of the Royal Commission on Indian Affairs, Volume 1, pp. 126-128 (British Columbia 1916; Interim Report No. 91). Ratification of the report by the province in 1924 constituted an official recognition of the treaty.

was the election of 1962). They also, in effect, have the same rights to the use of alcohol as other citizens. Liquor was prohibited to them until 1951, when the revised Indian Act made provision to permit them to drink in public drinking places, subject to provincial consent. A further amendment in 1956 allowed the provinces to remove all restrictions on the sale of liquor to Indians, and British Columbia did so in 1962. Technically, the possession of liquor on a reserve is still subject to a band plebiscite, but this provision is almost impossible to enforce because of the large number of bands. Potlatching and certain forms of winter ceremonies were prohibited by the old Indian Act, but when it was revised in 1951 these sections were left out. In matters not specifically covered by treaties or the Indian Act, Indians are subject to the ordinary provincial laws.

The title to Indian reserve land is vested in the (federal) crown, and such land is not subject to provincial legislation or zoning regulations. The Indians may not sell reserve land; they may, however, surrender it to the crown for sale on their behalf. No taxes are paid on reserve land, nor on the personal property of Indians on reserves. Real and personal property on reserves may not be mortgaged and are not subject to seizure, hence cannot be used as security for loans, a situation that the Indian Affairs Branch has tried to remedy by establishing a Revolving Loan Fund of $1,000,000 from which Indians may borrow for suitable purposes (see Finances, below). Indian income earned on the reserve is not taxable, but that earned off the reserve is subject to tax.

The division of the province into 20 Indian agencies, under the over-all supervision of the Indian Commissioner for British Columbia, has already been described (see Table 4 and Map 5). Each agency is administered by an Indian Superintendent and his staff. Within the agencies are the bands, each a distinct legal unit with its own band list of members, its own band funds, and its own reserves. Each band has a council, consisting of a chief ("chief councillor") and from two to twelve councillors, depending on its size, on the basis of one councillor for every hundred band members. The council is chosen by election or by the traditional custom of the band, whichever they wish, and serves for a two-year term. Women have the vote, and many are now serving as chiefs and councillors. The band councils exercise an increasing amount of control over the use of band funds and property, and over such aspects of reserve management as public works, traffic, weed control and health. They may not, however, decide on such important matters as the sale of reserve land without the approval of the Superintendent.

Finances

In addition to the expenditures of the Indian Affairs Branch for its operations and services (which totalled $9,264,339 in British Columbia during 1962-63) and those of the Indian and Northern Health Services and other government departments that give services to Indians, certain other funds are available to the Indians of the province. Chief among these are the "band funds" held in the Indian Trust Fund in Ottawa in the credit of the individual bands. These funds are derived largely from the lease and sale of reserve lands, and the sale of timber, gravel, or other resources of the reserves. They may be spent by the council on housing or any other purpose to the benefit of band members. When an Indian becomes enfranchised, he receives a per capita share of his band fund, and when a woman marries into another band, she takes her share with her. Two other sources of funds are also available. The British Columbia special grant of $100,000 per year in lieu of treaty payments may be used for irrigation projects or other improvements and equipment. The Revolving Loan Fund of $1,000,000 (for all of Canada) is a source from which Indians may borrow to obtain machinery, live stock, boats and other equipment.

Education

Although education in Canada is generally a provincial concern, the responsibility for the education of Indians is assumed by the Indian Affairs Branch. In 1962, the Branch maintained 70 day schools on reserves in the province, and supported or maintained 11 residential schools. The latter are operated by religious organizations, and their teachers follow the regular provincial

St Michael's Residential School, Alert Bay, in the mid 1950s. Wilson Duff photograph, RBCM PN3213.

curriculum. During 1962-63, 3,792 children attended Indian day schools and 2,169 attended residential schools. Of great and growing importance in recent years has been the development of joint (integrated) schools. The Branch enters into agreements with local school boards so that Indian children may attend the regular provincial schools, with the Branch paying the costs of their tuition, and in the case of new joint schools, a share of the construction costs as well. The number of Indian children attending provincial and private schools is growing rapidly; in 1962-63 it was 5,108 (Canada 1963, Department of Citizenship and Immigration, Table 29).

School attendance figures, like the population figures, have grown tremendously in recent years, and an increasing number of Indian students are reaching secondary and university levels or are taking vocational training. In January, 1963, 7 Indian students were enrolled in Grade 13, 10 at university level, and 100 in vocational programs (British Columbia 1962, p. 8). Programs of adult education are receiving increased attention. Leadership courses, homemakers' courses, rehabilitation and placement services, and other community projects are sponsored by the Indian Affairs Branch.*

Health and Welfare
As in the case of education, the federal government assumes what is normally a provincial responsibility in providing the Indians with health and welfare services, and there is a growing trend to obtain these services by contract from the existing provincial agencies. Medical treatment of Indians on reserves (and those who have lived off reserves for less than a year) is the responsibility of the Indian and Northern Health Services of the Department of National Health and Welfare, working in co-operation with the Indian Affairs Branch. A recent trend in some areas is to extend provincial and local public health nursing services to the reserves. Social welfare services for Indians are the responsibility of the Indian Affairs Branch. Indians living on reserves receive welfare payments from the Branch somewhat lower than the provincial scale. Indians living off reserves may obtain social assistance on the prevailing provincial scale from provincial or local welfare offices, and if the recipient has lived off the reserve for less than a year, the cost is borne by the Indian Affairs Branch. Indians may also obtain health services from the provincial or local offices if they have lived off the reserve for more than a year.

(Continuing negotiations between the federal and provincial governments suggest that this rather confusing division of services will continue to change. One might predict that eventually

---

* A new program of "community development" is now being initiated by the Indian Affairs Branch in cooperation with the provinces and local Indian communities. This approach supplements the existing programs of education, welfare and economic development, with the aim of making the best overall use of all available resources for the social and material development of the community. Among the communities where this new approach may prove effective is Port Simpson, where the first "community development consultant" in British Columbia will start work early in 1965.

all health and welfare services to Indians will be provided by provincial agencies at the same standards as prevail for non-Indians, with the Indian Affairs Branch paying the cost.*)

Indians receive Family Allowances, Old-age Security, Old-age Assistance, Disability and Blind Persons' Allowances, the same as other citizens. Child welfare services are provided by the provincial and private agencies with the cooperation of the Branch.

Indians and the Provincial Government

Although the federal government has jurisdiction over Indian lands and Indian affairs, the Indian people are full citizens of British Columbia in all important respects. They have the vote in provincial elections, and an Indian, Frank Calder, has held a seat in the Legislature (for all except one term) since 1950. Furthermore, as has been described, provincial agencies are becoming increasingly more involved in providing education, welfare and other services to the Indians.

In 1950, in an attempt to understand better the problems of its Indian citizens, the provincial government established an Indian Advisory Committee of six members (half of them Indians) and a secretary. Its purpose is to advise the government on "all matters regarding the status and rights of Indians". Annual reports have been published and annual meetings have dealt with a wide variety of topics. In 1963 this Committee was enlarged to nine members plus a director.

---

* Beginning January 1 1965, Indian Affairs Branch welfare payments to Indians will be given at the same scale and by the same procedures as for non-Indians, in preparation for transfer of the service to the provincial agencies. In addition, a pilot project will soon be initiated in the Okanagan Agency, whereby all welfare services to Indians will be provided by the provincial offices, with the Indian Affairs Branch paying the costs.

MORE CHANGES IN INDIAN LIFE

As British Columbia has grown from a sparsely settled fur-trading outpost to a complex industrial society, the impact of western civilization on the cultures of the Indians has been all but overwhelming. Cultures are integrated systems of belief and behaviour that tend to resist change. But some aspects of culture are less resistant to change than others. In general it is easier to change items of material culture and technology than it is to change non-material aspects such as attitudes and beliefs; the test of a new tool is its obvious utility, but there is no such easy test for a new belief. Habitual patterns of economic activity tend to resist change because they are usually linked with social customs and established rhythms of life. Social and religious beliefs and observances are most resistant of all, for they are set in deeply ingrained convictions about how the universe operates, and what is right and wrong. But since a culture is an integrated whole, a change in one aspect produces indirect changes in others. And resistance can be overcome by strong enough pressures. In the situation that followed the onrush of white settlement, drastic cultural change was inevitable. The Indians, by choice, adopted many new forms, starting chain-reactions of change within their own cultures. Added to that, forces in the dominant culture were applying strong pressures to destroy the old patterns and impose new ones. The question was not whether the Indians would change – it was whether in the end they would disappear as a distinct group in the population (assimilation), or would retain or create a subculture that could endure in some harmonious relationship with the larger culture (integration).

To put the question more bluntly: were the Indians on a non-stop one-way track to the white man's way of life? Did they want to be? We might gain a new perspective by looking for a moment, from the Indian point of view, at the civilization they found bearing ever more insistently on their lives. In some ways this new culture was obviously superior; in technology, for example, the choice was as simple as that between the diesel engine and the paddle. In other ways it was strange and alien. Its economy was based on concepts stemming from centuries of agricultural life;

these came to the Indians in the form of land-hungry settlers, new rules of land ownership, and the white man's conviction that nothing could be more natural for the Indian than to "turn to the plough" (or at least copy the vestigial farms that are part of all good European households in the form of neat, picket-fenced gardens). Their introduction to free enterprise was the "anything for a profit" of the maritime fur-trader and whisky-peddler. This particular period in history happened to find the British intolerant of cultural differences, prudish of morals, much impressed by their obvious superiority over the primitive races of the world, and bound with superhuman zeal to convert the heathen. The Indians, confused and sick, were no match for the men of massive courage and faith, massive theologies, and massive churches, who brought them Christianity. Human-itarianism is a British virtue, but it came to the Indians cloaked in the guise of unduly severe suppression of established cus-toms. The white man's social usages – for example, his system of personal names – were intrinsically no better than those of the Indians but came as part of the package, and it was the Indians who had to bear the inconvenience of the change-over. If the Indians were lacking in political institutions, the newcomers were not, and a political system based on that of Britain was soon established, within which the Indians had to find their place and learn the rules. There were obvious inconsistencies in the new way of life: in the difference between what was preached by the missionaries and what was practised by the sailors and loggers, and in the spectacle of church factions warring bitterly over which of them was to teach the Indians the lesson of peace and love. The culture being foisted on the Indians could hardly have appeared a pure mixture of blessings.

Will the answer be assimilation or integration? We cannot say, because the process of change has not yet run its course. What we see in Indian life today is not the old cultures in slightly modified forms, and it is not a carbon copy of the white man's culture. Nor has it settled into an equilibrium as a somewhat different sub-culture, which is what it might become. In technology and eco-nomic life a few vestiges of the old forms persist where these are useful, but by and large the Indians are adopting the new forms as rapidly as circumstances permit. In social life the old forms are also disappearing. Some traces remain in such things as the coastal Indians' love of sociability, respect for kinship ties and talent for speech-making, and some old patterns take on new vitality in the new situation, such as canoe races and spirit dance gatherings. In religion there is on the surface a willing acceptance of Christianity; below the surface; a few old forms such as shamanism and spirit dancing persist, but these are not considered religion. The need for political institutions has arisen from the need to exercise some control over their own destinies in the new circumstances, and new political structures are evolving: a government-sponsored system of bands and agencies, and a spontaneous growth of tribal and intertribal brotherhoods. In art, music, and dancing there is a conscious attempt to reaffirm an Indian identity by adapting old styles to new uses. On the whole it would seem that most Indians want to maintain an Indian culture and to find their identities as Indians. Whether this is a way-station on the road to conformity remains to be seen.

Material Culture

The material goods made and used by the Indians have changed so completely since the arrival of Europeans that most aboriginal forms may now be seen only in museums (which is one good reason for the existence of museums). A few modifications of such old forms as moccasins and dugout canoes still find occasional use in some of the Indian villages. But on the whole, the technology of the Indians was rendered obsolete and replaced by the technology of the white men. And as a general rule, the degree to which the Indians have adapted themselves to modern North American material culture is the degree to which they have been successful in finding their way in today's world.

The changes that began with the Nootkas bargaining eagerly with Captain Cook for pieces of iron gained momentum until the Indians had become almost wholly dependent on the whites for materials and manufactured goods. Metal cutting-blades replaced those of stone, bone and shell. The gun displaced the bow

and arrow, dagger and club. Tailored clothes and blankets replaced garments and robes of bark, wool and skin, and put an
end to the ancient techniques used in their manufacture. New
forms of fish-hooks replaced the old, as did new paints and dyes,
fire-making equipment, jewellery and so on. The paddle gave
way to the sail and the motor as the canoe was replaced by the
troller, gill-netter, seiner and packer. Other changes came with
the new social and religious life: on the coast the house type
changed from large multifamily dwellings to smaller types in the
European style, with windows, stoves, indoor plumbing, refrig-
erators and television sets.

Many things became obsolete and passed out of use: the
equipment and costumes of warriors and shamans; the masks,
robes, headdresses, rattles, drums, whistles and other paraphernalia of the potlatch and winter dance; the huge carved bowls,
ladles and spoons used in feasts; and totem poles. These old
things have quality and worth as the physical records of distinctive human ideas, skills and sensibilities; these are the things that
the museum has the role of preserving.

Since museums have been mentioned, something should be
said about the truly astonishing amount of Indian material from
this area that has found its way into the great museums of North
America and Europe. The material was abundant, artistic and
relatively portable, and it became available at a period when interest in the peoples and cultures of the world was growing, and
the great museums were being established.

The trend began with the earliest explorers: objects collected
on the Cook and Vancouver expeditions are now in the British
Museum and elsewhere in Europe. Fur traders of several coun-
tries took collections home; for example, the Yankee traders did
so, and the result is that many objects of great historical importance are now found in museums along the Atlantic seaboard.
Almost all scientific men who came to the coast assembled collections. The great Canadian geologist G.M. Dawson did so in
the late 1870s, and his collection is now in the Redpath Museum
in Montreal. The German geographer Aurel Krause studied the
Tlingit Indians in 1881 (Krause 1956) and took collections home
to Bremen. Another German, Capt. J. Adrian Jacobsen, made

extensive collections for the Royal Ethnographic Museum in Berlin. In 1885 he and his brother, B. Fillip Jacobsen, collected several tons of material at a cost of $16,000 on the coast, and took them to Berlin along with nine Bella Coola Indians who were to demonstrate their use (Victoria *Daily Colonist*, July 28 1885, p. 3).

It was these Indians who first interested the great Dr Franz Boas in the Northwest Coast, and the following year he made the first of his many visits to the area. He, too, was to make large collections for German and American institutions. Russian administrators in Alaska sent collections home, and these are now found in the museums of Russia and Finland. The first Indian Commissioner, Dr I.W. Powell, also took it upon himself to preserve Indian objects and send them to Ottawa. Lieut. George T. Emmons, an American officer, and Judge James G. Swan, of Port Townsend, were two of several Americans who became authorities on coastal Indian life and sent large collections to museums in the United States.

In Victoria, Dr C.F. Newcombe became a prodigious collector in the 1890s. He sent large collections to the Field Museum in Chicago, and also took a troupe of Indians to perform at the World's Columbian Exposition in 1898. Later he sent an extensive collection to the National Museum in Ottawa, and between 1911 and 1914 collected large amounts of excellent material for the Provincial Museum in Victoria. His son, W.A. Newcombe, was his constant companion and his successor, and continued to expand the family's private collection, which came to the Provincial Museum after his death in 1961.

The ethnologists who have worked in the area have also made large collections for museums. Notable among these are Harlan I. Smith (American Museum of Natural History and the National Museum of Canada), Marius Barbeau (National Museum of Canada) and James Teit (Provincial Museum and National Museum of Canada). There were also wealthy private collectors like George G. Heye, whose massive collections now form the Museum of the American Indian in New York, and Lord Alfred Bossom, whose large collection was recently returned from England to the National Museum of Canada. Missionaries, merchants and others made private collections, most of which are

Inside a house at 'Mi'mkwamlis in Kwakwaka'wakw (Kwakiutl) territory. Four feast dishes (two in the shape of wolves and two in the shape of Killer Whales) were collected by C.F. Newcombe for the British Columbia Provincial Museum. They remain in the museum's collection. C.F. Newcombe photograph, RBCM PN29.

now in museums; for example, the Raley and Collison collections in the University of British Columbia Museum of Anthropology, the Lipsett Collection at the Pacific National Exhibition in Vancouver, and the Rasmussen Collection in the Portland Art Museum. A number of sizeable collections are still in private hands.

Dr Erna Gunther has sought out and examined more of these far-flung Northwest Coast collections than anyone else, and she borrowed material from many of them to assemble an exhibit at the Seattle World's Fair in 1962. In her catalogue of the exhibit (Gunther 1962) she listed the collections she has seen. In Europe these included four in Britain, four in Germany, three in Switzerland, two in Russia, and one each in Denmark, Finland, Spain, Italy, Austria and France. In the United States there are extensive collections in Washington, New York, Chicago and Seattle, and smaller but important collections in Juneau, Portland, Denver, Brooklyn, Berkeley, Cambridge (Harvard University), New Haven (Yale University), Salem, Philadelphia, Milwaukee and elsewhere. In Canada the National Museum in Ottawa and the Provincial Museum in Victoria have major collections of about equal size and excellence, and other important collections are to be found in the Royal Ontario Museum (Toronto), the university and city museums in Vancouver, and the Redpath Museum in Montreal. Innumerable smaller collections are to be found elsewhere; almost all museums of importance have some Northwest Coast material.

The major collections of original totem poles are still in this area, at Victoria, Vancouver and Prince Rupert. But numbers of poles were shipped by early collectors like Newcombe and Barbeau to distant museums. Collections of half a dozen or more are to be found in Ottawa, Toronto, Washington, Chicago and New York, and smaller numbers are scattered through England, in Paris, Bremen, Stockholm, Denver, Berkeley, Milwaukee, Montreal, Quebec, Jasper and elsewhere.

This great export of Northwest Coast material to the museums of the world has often been deplored by people in British Columbia. But most of it was done before there was very much local interest or support for the preservation of such objects, and if the material had not been exported, most of it would have been destroyed.

A few vestiges of the material aspects of the old ways of life may still be observed. In coastal villages the houses may be set in a row parallel to the beach as in former times, and though they are of modern types, they usually lack the fenced gardens and neat painted exteriors favoured by people of agricultural backgrounds. Small utility dugouts may litter the beach, though the larger, more graceful canoes of the past are gone. There may be smokehouses for curing fish, and racks on which seaweed and herring-spawn are set out to dry. On a few old sites are decayed remnants of huge old house frames and totem poles, or rectangular depressions where old houses stood. In interior villages, smokehouses, meat caches, dip-nets or the occasional rack on which a Moose or bear hide is stretched for scraping may be seen, and some of the people may be wearing moccasins. Otherwise, Indian villages show little indication that they are "Indian", and usually disappoint tourists intent on photographing Indian life.

Some parts of the present Indian material culture might better be termed neo-Indian because it has no exact counterpart in the old local culture. The slim and beautiful racing canoes of the Coast Salish (and canoe racing itself) are direct modifications of old forms. The costumes, headdresses and other properties of modern Indian dancing troupes may have some resemblance to those of the past, but often they borrow heavily from Plains costumes or Hollywood versions of Indian costumes. We sometimes deplore their lack of authenticity, but they do represent an honest attempt to affirm a clear identity as Indians.

Arts and Crafts

Indian arts and crafts are present-day products that have evolved directly or indirectly from old native forms, products that have enjoyed a continued development because of a demand for them in the larger culture. White men have been buying useful Indian wares and curios since the time of first contact, and continue to do so. Although these are removed from their original native contexts, they still satisfy real needs. Handicrafts such as baskets still find uses in the modern home. Indian arts such as wood carving are much in demand by modern interior decorators. Their appeal lies partly in their identification with the Indians and with the local region, but it is also the appeal of skilled hand-craftsmanship in an age of standardized machine-made products. Most of these crafts have evolved a long way from their aboriginal prototypes; many of them (beadwork, silverwork, argillite carving, knitting) are not aboriginal at all, but of mixed Indian-white origin. Since it is in the larger culture that these crafts are actually used, and since the demand from the larger culture influences their forms, they are just as much products of the material culture of modern North America as they are products of Indian culture.

The special skills that have persisted or developed from the old Indian cultures fall into two groups: handicrafts, which are usually the work of women; and Indian art, which is usually the work of men. There is a tendency for some of the more difficult and time-consuming skills, such as basketry and weaving, to be relinquished with the passing of the older generation, but other skills such as carving, painting and knitting seem to be more than holding their own. In practically every part of the province, Indians add to their cash incomes by practising one or other of these skills as a full- or part-time occupation. Conscious attempts have been made by non-Indians to preserve and stimulate native arts and crafts. In 1939 in Victoria the Society for the Furtherance of B.C. Indian Arts and Crafts (later changed to B.C. Indian Arts and Welfare Society) was established, and its founder, Dr Alice Ravenhill, published a book of designs called *A Cornerstone of Canadian Culture* (Ravenhill 1944). This organization and others, such as the Canadian Handicrafts Guild, have maintained a constant interest in native crafts. It seems to be generally agreed that these skills could yield much higher returns to the Indian people

A Lillooet basket maker, 1906. RBCM PN6575.

if more efficient procedures were introduced to procure raw materials in bulk, give instruction to craftsmen, educate the buying public and improve marketing arrangements (cf. Hawthorn et al. 1958, pp. 257-267). Some non-Indian retailers have found it good business to assist Indian craftsmen along these lines. The Indians themselves have been less successful in trying to organize the production and sale of crafts, and to date they have had little in the way of assistance from the Indian Affairs Branch or other government agencies.

The arts and crafts that now contribute significantly to Indian income are the following: basketry and weaving; skinwork and beadwork; birchbark baskets; the Cowichan knitting industry; argillite carving; silverwork; jade jewellery; wood carving and painting; and totem-pole restoration projects. (See also Hawthorn et al. 1958, pp. 257-267.)

Basketry and Weaving

All the Interior Salish tribes, and also the Chilcotin, Sechelt, Squamish, Stalo and adjacent tribes in Washington State, formerly made firm coiled baskets of cedar-root splints decorated by imbrication with bleached grass and wild-cherry bark (for an exhaustive study of the craft, see Haeberlin et al. 1928). The baskets were made in a limited number of shapes for specific uses: wedge-shaped burden baskets, oblong cradles, round or nut-shaped baskets for holding water or cooking, small pot-shaped baskets for food storage, and large rectangular forms for other storage. Later, when they were made for sale, a great variety of forms evolved: all manner of shapes with handles, lids and looped rims, also trays, place-mats, rattles and even tables. A few women, especially among the Thompson and Lillooet, still make baskets in this technique for sale. But the amount of labour involved in digging and splitting the roots and weaving the baskets is great, and the wage to the craftswoman is small. Younger women find little incentive to take up the craft. Probably the volume of production will continue to decline until these fine baskets become collector's items, when the craft will enjoy a revival.

The Nootka tribes wove hats and small baskets of cedar bark and bleached or dyed swamp grass in a technique known as wrapped twining. A number of forms came to be made for sale: trinket baskets, shopping baskets, and bottles or shells covered with basketry. A number of women on the west coast of Vancouver Island still make these for the market. Farther north on the coast, the Tlingit and some Haida made somewhat similar baskets of fine spruce roots, woven in simple twining and decorated with dyed grass in false embroidery.* A few Tlingit women in Alaska still make these baskets, as do a few Haida women at Masset.

Blankets woven of Mountain Goat wool and Yellow-cedar bark were distinctive products of coastal Indian technology, but are no longer made. Mrs Mungo Martin was the last to make the famous Chilkat robes (although a few Alaskan women still have the knowledge and skill). Cedar-bark mats and bags, formerly so common, have also passed out of use. All of these crafts could still be revived.

Skinwork and Beadwork

All the interior tribes used deer, Moose or Caribou hides to make shirts, leggings, dresses, moccasins, headdresses and other clothing. These items were often decorated with painted designs, shells, or dyed porcupine quills. With the introduction of glass beads and the technique of embroidery, the decoration of buckskin clothing and containers was brought to the level of a fine art. Today these tribes produce considerable numbers of moccasins, slippers, vests, jackets and gloves. These are often tanned an attractive white colour or smoked to an orange hue, and decorated with fringes, beading and embroidery. In addition, they make a variety of other beaded items for the tourist market, including souvenir belts, small brooches in the form of dolls or gloves, and decorated cushions.

---

* The most convenient publications on basketry construction and decoration techniques are the Denver Art Museum (n.d.) Indian Leaflet Series, nos 67 and 68.

Birchbark Baskets
The Athapaskans and Interior Salish used birchbark to make dishes, ladles and a variety of storage baskets. These were cut into patterns, folded into shape, sewn with strips of willow, rimmed with a wooden hoop sewn on with willow twigs or quills, and decorated with etched designs. The craft is still carried on by women of a number of interior bands, especially in the Hazelton and Burns Lake areas, and useful and attractive baskets may still be obtained at reasonable prices.

The Cowichan Knitting Industry
The Salish of Vancouver Island and the Fraser Valley as far up-river as Lytton now knit heavy water-resistant sweaters, tams, socks and mitts of raw sheep's wool. This growing Indian industry takes its name from the Cowichan tribe, which has always been the centre of its development. In addition to being warm, the garments are distinctive in appearance, usually with a white or grey background and a black design. They are eagerly sought by outdoor sportsmen, and the demand far exceeds the supply. One Victoria dealer alone sells about 6,000 sweaters each year, worth almost $120,000 to the knitters.

Knitting is not an aboriginal technique, but the Coast Salish do have a background in the working of wool. They formerly spun the hair of the Mountain Goat and a special breed of dog into a coarse yarn and wove it into blankets on a two-bar loom. One may still occasionally see an older woman spinning with the old form of hand spindle, but most women now use a machine adapted from the treadle sewing machine. Sweaters are knitted "in the round" on as many as eight needles, producing a seamless garment. The technique betrays its place of origin; it was used in northern Scotland and taught to the Indians by early Scottish settlers on Vancouver Island. The decorative designs are sometimes simple geometric forms similar to aboriginal basketry decoration, but more often are complex embroidery designs showing bird, animal or other forms. (See Lane 1951 for a more complete description of this craft.)

Argillite Carving

The sculpture of "black slate" is one of the best-known art forms of the Haida of the Queen Charlotte Islands, and was the first form made entirely for the curio trade. By about 1820 the fur trade was declining because of a scarcity of Sea Otters, and the Haida began to offer other products for sale. One of these was potatoes, which by then they were growing in large quantities; another was curios, mainly argillite carvings. They were accomplished artists of long standing in the sculpture of wood, horn and stone, and the distinctive Haida art style was already well developed. Yet in their earliest attempts at argillite carving they seem to have been influenced by the scrimshaw carvings of the white seafaring men. They made platters and pipes and flutes

An elaborate example of argillite carving. Three-dimensional figures emerge from all sides of this chest: on the front, a bird with recurved beak; on the back, a beaver's head; and on each end, a bear. The lid tableau illustrates the creation myth in which Raven released mankind from a cockle shell. The chest's feet are frogs. Carved by Charles Edenshaw (1839-1920). RBCM CPN10622.

decorated with the white men's geometric and floral patterns, and figures of white sea captains in uniform (sometimes with white faces carved separately of bone), and complex unsmokeable panel pipes showing ships and men and the occasional ship's pet. These early carvings, dating from about 1820 to the 1860s, are now prized museum pieces. Most of the carvers, even in the early period, drew heavily from Haida art and mythology for their designs, and the white men's motifs were soon entirely supplanted, even on the pipes, plates, elaborate boxes and candleholders, by Haida animal and human designs. Single figures and panels of figures became popular, and most popular of all became the model totem poles, which form the backbone of most recent collections of argillite.

For the past generation or two this art form has been at a low ebb. Today about half a dozen carvers at Skidegate make model poles, brooches, ashtrays and other items, which are mostly sold in craft shops in Victoria, Vancouver and Prince Rupert. The craftsmanship is often very good, but the artistic standards of the work are generally below those of former generations of carvers. The present carvers find difficulty in obtaining suitable pieces of slate for carving. The only source is a single rock-slide quarry on the side of a mountain some distance from Skidegate, legally reserved for the use of the Skidegate band. Someone pulverized much of the supply with a dynamite charge a few years ago, in an attempt to dislodge larger chunks from the slide. The popularity of primitive art in recent decades has been felt in a greatly increased demand for argillite carvings both old and new, and a corresponding increase in their price. The demand has been met in part with cast replicas, the best of which are distributed by a few large American museums. Recent publications have also made this art form more widely known (e.g., Barbeau 1953 and 1957).

Silverwork
The working of silver into jewellery is said to have been introduced to the northern coast tribes by the Russians at Sitka, from whom it spread to the Tlingit and Haida, and to a lesser extent to the other coast tribes. Like argillite, it was probably influenced by the scrimshaw work of the Yankee sailors, but soon came to

be a new medium for beautiful representations of Indian designs. The best silverworkers were among the Haida, the same artists usually working in both silver and argillite, and often wood as well. Silver dollars provided the raw material, and these were beaten into bracelets, brooches, spoons and other forms, and incised with Northwest Coast designs (for more information on the development of the craft see Barbeau 1939).

Today there are only about half a dozen Indian silverworkers scattered along the length of the coast of British Columbia. With one exception, their output is small and the quality of their work is less than excellent. The one exception is Bill Reid of Vancouver, the outstanding Haida artist of this generation. For several years he has been making silver and gold jewellery that brings the classic Haida art style to new levels of perfection. Reid is a grandson of Charles Gladstone, the last of the older generation of Haida silverworkers. He did not grow up in an Indian environment, and developed an interest in modern and primitive art and a skill in modern jewellery-making before discovering the art style of his Haida forebears. Then, in silver, gold, and wood, he gave the style expression that was at the same time conventional and modern (see also page 125).

Jade Jewellery
Within the last few years lapidary work with local jade has become a significant Indian craft in the Lytton and Lillooet area, centring on St Michael's Residential School (see the photograph on page 103). This modern craft also has some roots in the past, because for many centuries, jade from this area was made into polished adze blades and traded to tribes over a large part of the coast and interior.

Wood Carving and Painting
The coastal Indians have, of course, been master wood-carvers for many centuries, and the art style they evolved was essentially a wood-carvers' style. Most objects of Northwest Coast art were of carved and painted wood: totem poles, canoes, masks, rattles, staffs, dishes, spoons and so on. It is not surprising that something of this emphasis has persisted, and that a large proportion

of the objects made for sale by the coastal tribes today are of wood.

The totem pole has attained the status of the symbol or trademark of the entire area, and totems, large and small, good and bad, are the most common of the objects made. Full-sized poles are seldom attempted except in formal programs of totem pole restoration, but a few individual carvers accept contracts for poles from 5 to 15 feet (1.5 to 5 metres) in height. Small models ranging in size from a few inches to 2 feet (up to 60 cm) are made by the thousand: these formed no part of the aboriginal cultures but originated in response for the demand for curios; some (mostly Kwakiutl) reveal fine craftsmanship in an established tribal art style; but most represent the individual styles of carvers of the southern coast tribes who had little or no traditional background of totem poles, and are "garish and meaningless little souvenirs" (Hawthorn et al. 1958, p. 259). The talented Indian

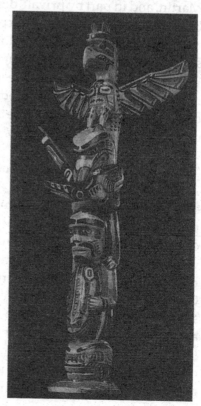

A model pole carved by Charlie James. It features, from top to bottom, a thunderbird, a bear with a whale in its mouth, a man holding a frog, and a head. RBCM CPN6787.

carver has to choose between volume production of low-priced souvenir poles (called "idiot sticks" by some) and works of high quality that must be sold for high prices. The demand for excellence is growing, and the few carvers who develop their own skills to the point where they are producing fine works of sculpture are also in effect extending their own tribal traditions.

Masks are also carved in large numbers for sale, and are often finished in plain modern styles (sometimes sand-blasted to emphasize the grain of the wood) rather than painted in the old fashion. Feast dishes, spoons, paddles, plaques and single-animal figures are also made in numbers and, like masks, make striking furnishings for modern interiors.

The painting of Indian designs on paper, fabrics or wooden panels has enjoyed a recent revival among Kwakiutl artists. This was stimulated in part by sets of paintings done for the Provincial Museum and the University of British Columbia by Mungo Martin, and in part by private dealers in Vancouver. The effect has been the production of a surprising variety of designs that, though not slavish copies of old designs, are purely Kwakiutl in style. Though times have changed, that style is still evolving.

Indian designs have also been adapted by non-Indian craftsmen for the decoration of wooden and ceramic bowls and other objects. Some of these are quite attractive, but most (especially in ceramics) lose something of the character of the original designs.

Totem-Pole Restoration Projects

A large totem pole carved by a skilled craftsman in one of the established tribal art styles is an imposing monument, one of the peaks of human achievement in wood sculpture. As such, many of them have been collected by the museums of the world and will be preserved indoors indefinitely. In addition, the totem pole has become a tourist attraction and symbol of west-coast Canadian life, and as such there has been added incentive to preserve numbers of them here in their home area. Most such attempts have been in outdoor settings, and little more than delaying actions against the forces of decay. The emphasis is now on moving the original poles indoors and using newly carved replicas or original poles for outdoor exhibits.

The Haida and coastal Tsimshian stopped carving totem poles for their own use in the 1880s, and the Niska and other north-coast tribes did the same a decade or two later. Only a few de-cayed remnants may still be found in these areas, and the poles collected for outdoor restoration are also in advanced states of decay. The Gitksan of the upper Skeena area continued to carve poles until about 1950, but the quality of the art style has been on the decline since the turn of the century (Duff 1952b). In the vil-lages of that area a few dozen poles still exist that are good enough and sound enough to be preserved. At Alert Bay and other Southern Kwakiutl villages, totem poles continued to be carved and the art style continued to develop until a generation ago. This is the style represented by Mungo Martin, which is being developed further by Henry Hunt in Victoria and Doug Cranmer in Vancouver. Old poles representing earlier stages in this style now stand in Stanley Park and at the University of British Columbia in Vancouver, and more recent poles may still be seen in numbers at Alert Bay.

The first major outdoor restoration project in British Columbia was undertaken in 1925 and 1926 in the upper Skeena villages of Kitwanga and Kitselas by the Canadian government and the Canadian National Railway (see Barbeau 1950, pp. 849ff.). Indian labour, under the direction of Harlan I. Smith of the National Museum and a railway engineer, was employed to take down the old poles, oil and repaint them, and erect them facing the road or railway on new cedar poles set in concrete bases. About 18 poles were restored at Kitwanga and 10 at Kitselas. By 1962, several of the Kitwanga poles had been destroyed by fire or had fallen down again, and few were sound enough for further restoration, and all the poles at Kitselas were decayed beyond hope of further preservation.

In Vancouver, the Art, Historical and Scientific Association during the 1920s undertook to build a model Indian village at Lumbermen's Arch in Stanley Park. Four Kwakiutl poles were erected as a nucleus in 1926, and two additional Kwakiutl and one Haida pole were added ten years later. Although the aim of building lodges was not achieved, this group of poles has re-mained an outstanding exhibit. In 1962 they were taken down;

the Haida pole was recopied and the others extensively repaired by Doug Cranmer and Bill Reid, and set up in a new location.

During the 1930s and 1940s, about a dozen Haida poles and two Nass River poles were assembled in Prince Rupert and erected in city parks. These, too, formed fine exhibits until further decay began to reduce their numbers over the past few years. In 1963 and 1964, William Jefferies, a local carver, was employed to make copies of the old poles, and six of the originals were sent to the Provincial Museum for permanent preservation.

Thunderbird Park, the outdoor totem pole exhibit of the Provincial Museum in Victoria, was established in 1941. Haida, Kwakiutl, Bella Coola, Nootka and Coast Salish poles were placed on display and also a number of canoes. By 1952, it had become evident that the old poles were continuing to decay, and it was decided to replace them with replicas and new exhibits. Mungo Martin was brought to Victoria, and a carving program started, and still continues. Over the years almost all of the exhibits have been replaced; the old poles have been returned to storage and a new series of more representative displays created (see Duff 1963 and the Annual Reports of the British Columbia Provincial Museum). The exhibits are arranged in groups by tribe, and in the centre is a complete Kwakiutl house. This was designed by Mungo Martin and opened by him with full ceremony in 1953, and has been the scene of several Indian dances and other functions since then.

Mungo Martin continued as chief carver until his death in 1962, when he was succeeded by his protégé, Henry Hunt. Over the years it has been possible to maintain one additional carver in training, but the original aim of establishing an apprenticeship program has not yet been achieved. The continuing program* has, however, permitted the production of totem poles for dis-

---

* Note for the new edition: As of 1990, the Royal British Columbia Museum no longer has a resident-staff carving program in Thunderbird Park. It now offers a diverse range of programs with partners, such as the Victoria Native Friendship Centre, providing opportunities for aboriginal people to present their own interpretations of their culture and history.

play elsewhere than in the park. These now stand at several places in the province, and as far afield as Ottawa, London, Mexico City and Buenos Aires. Of special interest has been the arrangement between the Provincial Museum and the Gitksan village of Kitwancool, whereby the Museum has received four of the finest old poles in return for exact copies. As part of the arrangement, the Museum published the histories of the poles and of the tribe (Duff 1959).

An active program of totem-pole restoration was begun in 1947 at the University of British Columbia in Vancouver. Mungo Martin was retained to repair and paint a number of older Kwakiutl poles that had been assembled, and to carve two orig- inals. These were erected in an attractive wooded setting on the campus. In 1954 the Provincial Museum, with assistance from private and business sources, salvaged six Haida poles from Tanoo and Skedans, three of which were sent to the University for storage. This was the first of a series of such joint Museum- University projects: in 1956 several Kwakiutl poles were salvaged from four villages, and in 1957 an expedition removed the sal- vageable poles from the Haida village of Ninstints on Anthony Island (Duff and Kew 1958). The Haida poles stored at the University provided the basis for a Haida section in the totem park. Between 1960 and 1962, with the aid of Canada Council grants, the University commissioned Bill Reid and Doug Cran- mer to create a section of a Haida village. This consists of a mas- sive house, complete with a frontal pole and an inside house post, a smaller mortuary house with a frontal pole, a memorial pole, memorial figure, and two types of mortuary poles. The poles were designed by Bill Reid, working from the old poles in storage and from old photographs. They are not exact replicas, but are beautiful new poles within the old Haida tradition, and form one of the most impressive exhibits of massive wood sculp- ture in existence.*

---

* For another summary of totem pole restoration projects, including those in Alaska, see Keithahn 1963, pp. 113-130.

New Economic Directions

The native systems for the production of food and wealth were based on fishing, hunting and gathering; the systems for their distribution involved trade with other tribes and social mechanisms such as the potlatch, the feast and patterned gift exchanges between relatives. The impact of the white man has put an end, or nearly so, to these old systems, and replaced them, though not yet completely, with a new economic framework. Most Indian groups still obtain some proportion of their food by fishing, hunting and gathering, but very rarely is that their sole or principal source of subsistence. The Indians have adopted new occupations, or new variations of old ones, to produce goods for sale or to earn wages. Their entry into the money economy has changed the manner in which they distribute their wealth, and has been accompanied by the decay of old social mechanisms and the growth of new ones. They have entered the larger economic system but not yet become fully adapted to it; meanwhile the system itself is becoming more complex, making the problem of catching up doubly difficult.

Some of the early changes wrought by the fur trade have already been described. A new wealth of new goods was injected into the Indians' economy in exchange for furs, which they could obtain by spending a little more time hunting and trading, and their economy prospered. There were other benefits as well. The early introduction of potato cultivation along the coast provided a source of food much superior to the laborious digging of wild roots, and also provided a product that could be traded to the white men in quantity (Suttles 1951). In fact, there were several things the whites would buy in addition to furs: game, fish, shellfish, Indian curios, and not least, the services of women. In overall effect, the changes that came with the fur trade stimulated the native economy without disrupting it.

White settlement and the adoption of the money economy brought disruptive changes to the Indian economic patterns. Slowly and irreversibly (though not yet completely), traditional hunting and fishing rights have been curtailed. The Indians turned to new occupations that were based on traditional activities or in some other way congenial to their way of life. Some shipped aboard sealing vessels as hunters; others served as sailors or pilots; others as packers or guides. Trapping remained important, though subject to the ups and downs of a fickle market. The demand for Indian curios grew into a considerable business in arts and crafts, and the sale of old ethnological specimens and information to collectors added considerably to many Indian incomes. At times there were short-lived demands for single products, such as dogfish oil, which was used in huge quantities by early loggers to grease their skids. When Indians tried their hands at the extraction and sale of logs and agricultural products, they met with some initial success. Several Kwakiutl hand loggers, for example, carried on profitable operations at the turn of the century. Changes in the regulations put them out of business (Codere 1950, p. 39). Changes in technology would soon have done the same thing. In some areas, such as the Cowichan Valley, the Indians had early successes with agriculture, but increased competition by local white farmers and changes in the industry soon discouraged them. In some ways it seems to have been easier for the Indians of two or three generations ago to adjust to the simpler white economy of that time than it is for their grandsons to find a place in the more complex economy of today.

It is as wage-earners in industries some way related to their former pursuits that the Indians have been able to enter most fully into the modern economy. Foremost among these is commercial fishing and cannery work, employing more than a third of the wage-earning Indians of the province, mostly from the coast and upper Skeena bands. They work in every capacity, from cannery hands to captains of large vessels. Indians have played an important role in the fishing industry of the coast since its beginning. It was as a collective bargaining agent for the Indian fishermen that the Native Brotherhood developed its strength, during turbulent days in the history of the industry (see Jamieson and Gladstone 1950, Gladstone 1953 and Drucker 1958). Farming and ranching, mostly in the southern interior, ranks second in contributing to Indian income. Logging and sawmill work employ almost as many as farming, and are concentrated on the southern coast and in the central interior. Trapping, though still important, employs a relatively small number as compared with former times; these tend to be in the northern and central interior regions. Seasonal and migratory work, such as the picking of fruit and hops, draws considerable numbers of Indians to the Fraser Valley and southern interior, and to the adjacent United States. Guiding, packing and casual labour also employ numbers in the interior. Although few Indians have yet succeeded in professions or in private business, progress toward these goals in recent years has been relatively rapid. The increased mechanization of logging, fishing and farming, requiring more expensive equipment and higher levels of technical education, is making it doubly difficult for Indians to keep pace in these industries.

Religious Change: Conversion to Christianity

By 1904, 90 per cent of the Indians of the province were nominally Christian. In 1939 the census could number only 28 who still held to "aboriginal beliefs" (a few Tahltans and the rest Nootkas); at that time, 57 per cent of the Indians were Roman Catholic, 20 per cent Anglican, 20 per cent United Church and 3 per cent "other Christian beliefs" (mostly Salvation Army). Such a rapid and complete conversion is perhaps what one might expect in view of the strong determination of the missionaries of the past century to save heathen souls, but it could also be said that, in most areas, Indian resistance to the remaking of their lives was weaker than might be expected. Unsettled by the first effects of white contact, they often seemed hungry for new religious guidance. Even before the missionaries appeared in person, native "prophets" who had gained some garbled inklings of Christian beliefs and rituals found avid audiences for their teachings.

Apart from brief contacts along the coast in the course of the maritime fur trade, the first missionaries to reach the area were Roman Catholic priests from Quebec and France. During the

1840s, working from Fort Vancouver, Fort Langley and Fort Victoria, they reached the tribes of the southern coast and interior and made visits north into New Caledonia as well. By 1870 they were well established in these areas. Strangely, they met strong resistance to their mission among the Nootka, and utter failure in their mission among the Kwakiutl, and they did not venture among the tribes farther up the coast. Anglican missionaries from the Church Missionary Society in London were the first into the field on the northern coast, and centred their activities during the 1860s and 1870s at William Duncan's model community of Metlakatla. They also became established among the Kwakiutl around Alert Bay and won away from the Catholics the Thompson Indians around Lytton. Methodists from eastern Canada reached the Indians in the 1860s; working from Nanaimo they won some formerly Catholic communities on southeastern Vancouver Island and in the Fraser Valley, and from Victoria they extended their ministry up the coast to villages not yet served by Anglican missions. The northern coast and upper Skeena became an uneasy patchwork of Anglican and Methodist villages, and the appearance on the scene of the Salvation Army about the turn of the century added further to the interdenominational frictions. Since 1940 the Pentecostal Church has also become active in the area, as in other parts of the province.

The adoption of Christianity was not accomplished without the carrying over of a number of old beliefs and practices that are religious in the broader sense of the word. These continue to colour the Indians' Christian beliefs but do not conflict with them. An interesting by-product of the transition to Christianity was the formation of the Shaker Church, a Christian church with an Indian founder, its own Indian clergy, and an all-Indian congregation.

Prophet Cults
Some concepts of Christianity preceded the missionaries into most areas of the province, carried by "prophets" who foretold the arrival of white men and the marvels they would bring. These mystics are said to have gained their knowledge through

visions or by dying and returning to life after an instructive visit to heaven. They travelled among the tribes and harangued them, instructing their followers, for example, to make the sign of the cross, observe the Sabbath, worship a supreme being and publicly confess their sins. The early blends of Christian and native beliefs they taught make it very difficult for us now to determine what the purely aboriginal beliefs were. Most Indians today, for example, are convinced that their forebears worshipped a supreme being equivalent to the Christian God, but among most tribes such was probably not the case.

Traditions of these prophets have been recorded from the Coast Salish, the Interior Salish, the tribes of the upper Skeena and the Haida. Christian elements seem to have reached the Interior Salish first, and to have become integrated there into the ceremony known as the Prophet Dance, an aboriginal ritual that was peculiarly suited for the incorporation of Christian ideas. The Christianized Prophet Dance then spread to the other tribes, carrying a curious blend of Interior Salish and Christian ideas. By then, too, the first priests were reaching parts of the area, and local prophets had a new and more direct source of Christian concepts from which to fashion their short-lived creeds.

The Interior Salish Prophet Dance, in aboriginal times, seems already to have contained such elements as the worship of some sort of a deity, the inspired leader or prophet, and the public confession of sins (Suttles 1957). It also included a circular dance, in which the entire community participated, and a marriage dance. Its main purpose was to hasten the end of the world and the return of the dead to their living relatives. By the 1820s certain elements had been added that were clearly of Christian origin – the sign of the cross and the observance of a Sabbath. The probable source of these concepts was a pair of Indian youths who had been taken to the Red River settlement in 1825 and returned in 1829 to preach their newly learned religion. It was during the 1830s that the Christianized Prophet Dance spread to the Coast Salish. The feature of it that they remember best is the marriage dance, although it was fashionable with them for only a short period because it permitted marriages between high- and low-class people. The dance had several local forms, but typically the young men and women danced in a circle and chose partners by linking arms, or by placing a stick or feather on the other's shoulder, after which they were considered married.

They do not remember that the concept of a supreme deity was introduced at that time, though linguistic evidence indicates that it was. The deity worshipped in the Christianized Prophet Dance was called by a name derived from the French pronunciation of Jesus Christ. Coast Salish groups who do not remember this name refer to the deity by a name that translates into "Chief Above", and this is an exact equivalent of the term for God, used by missionaries and Indians, in Chinook jargon: "*Saghalie Tyee*".

While Catholic priests were instructing the tribes they were able to reach, prophets continued to appear in outlying areas, and founded cults based on a larger admixture of Christian elements. One such prophet appeared in the 1840s in the Fraser Valley near Agassiz (Duff 1952a, p. 121). While hunting in the mountains he is said to have met three men who told him to kneel, make the sign of the cross, and pray. When he opened his eyes he saw a large church inside the mountain, lighted with the brightest of colours. The men taught him the rules of conduct that would please God, and described stoves, matches and other marvels the white men would bring. They said that black-robed priests would soon arrive, who would be half good and half bad. Afterwards this prophet travelled up and down the valley and preached until the first white men came.

Another prophet, the best known of several in his tribe, was Bini, of the Bulkley River Carrier (Jenness 1943). He is said to have died, ascended to heaven and then returned to life. He taught his followers to say prayers, make the sign of the cross and observe a Sabbath, and he introduced public confession and purification by whipping. He foretold the arrival of marvels like flour and horses. He travelled about and preached, causing waves of excitement downriver to the coast and through the northern interior. Bini died a second and final time about 1870.

In the American Plateau to the south, further cults developed, with more of a nativistic, anti-white trend. One of these was the Smohalla cult of the Columbia River, whose members believed that by their rituals the white man would be destroyed and the old way of life would be restored. From such cults grew the anti-white Ghost Dance of the Plains. Similar cults, though without the anti-white trend, probably contributed to the origin of the Shaker Church.

Early Catholics

The first Spanish ships to explore the Northwest Coast had Catholic priests aboard, and the short-lived (1789-95) Spanish settlement at Nootka Sound included a Catholic church (Morice 1910). The Russian settlement at Sitka, first established in 1799, also brought priests to this general area. These early contacts seem not to have produced any profound impact on native beliefs.

Early in the 1840s Oblate and Jesuit missionaries from the east reached the southern coast and interior and penetrated north into New Caledonia. The first to arrive were Fathers N.F. Blanchet and Modeste Demers, Oblates from Quebec, who reached Fort Vancouver on the lower Columbia in 1838. In 1841 Father Demers visited Fort Langley for a week and found the Indians avid for instruction. From contacts with the tribes of Puget Sound they already knew the sign of the cross and a few simple hymns. "I was continually surrounded by fifteen to sixteen hundred adult savages," he wrote, "understanding my instructions, all listening attentively and with an incredible order." He baptized more than 400 during his stay (McKelvie 1947, p. 62). In 1843 another Oblate from Quebec, Father John Bolduc, accompanied James Douglas when he established Fort Victoria. He baptized 102 children and preached to the Songhees and neighbouring tribes. The southern interior was visited as early as 1840 by the Jesuit Father P.J. DeSmet, who for many years was to work among the Kootenay, Okanagan and Shuswap. New Caledonia was visited first by Father Demers, who went there in 1842 from Fort Vancouver with the fur brigade, preaching to the tribes along the way, and returning the next year. In 1845 and 1846, Father John Nobili, a Jesuit, travelled into the region, visiting all the Carrier tribes as far west as Babine Lake. Following his return in 1847, a dozen years were to pass before another priest reached the area (during which time an abundance of native prophets held the stage). In 1869, there arrived Father Jean Lejacq, a remarkable man who until 1885 served the vast area bounded by Hagwilget, Fort Connolly (Bear Lake), Fort McLeod and Fort St George. His successor was the even more remarkable Father Morice.

During the 1850s Victoria became an important centre of Catholic missionary endeavours. Modeste Demers was installed as the first Bishop of Vancouver Island in 1851, and priests were sent to the Indians of Saanich, Cowichan and the Fraser Valley. In 1859, Father C.M. Pandosy was sent to establish a mission in the Okanagan. Two years later, St Mary's Mission was established on the Fraser River above New Westminster, and this soon became the main centre of activity on the mainland and the site of an industrial school. Seldom did Catholic missionaries acknowledge failure, but one such instance was St Michael's Mission, established in 1863 among the Kwakiutl of Fort Rupert. Despite the efforts of the most able priests available, the mission made no headway and was abandoned in 1874. Difficulties were also encountered among the Northern Nootka, where Father Brabant founded the Hesquiat Mission in 1875. Many years of patient effort were required to bring these people into the church. No serious efforts were made to establish missions among the tribes farther up the coast or west of the Bulkley River in the northern interior.

Black-robed Roman Catholic priests at the Mission, Fraser Valley, 1868. The early missionaries in the interior and on the southern coast were Catholic. Frederick Dally photograph, RBCM PN8876.

The year 1880 saw the arrival from France of A.G. Morice, a man of forceful personality and powerful intellect who was to become the best known of the Catholic priests who served in British Columbia. Ordained in 1882 at St Mary's Mission, he was sent first to Williams Lake to work among the Shuswap and Chilcotin, then in 1885 was transferred to Fort St James to replace Father Lejacq. For 19 years he dominated the northern interior, and became an outstanding authority on its history, geography and native peoples. The list of his published works is long, and includes many studies of the Carrier Indians and the broader Déné or Athapaskan stock to which they belong (e.g., Morice 1895), a two-volume study of the Carrier language (1932), definitive histories of the northern interior (1904) and of the Catholic Church in western Canada (1910, 1923), and many more, both in English and in French. Not the least of his accomplishments was the invention of a simple syllabic script that could be used to write down Carrier and related languages. Canadian Athapaskan tribes over a wide area learned this script and used it to write letters or leave messages along the trail, and it was also cast into type and used in readers, prayer and hymn books, and a monthly periodical (Morice 1910, p. 377). This was not the only attempt by a Catholic priest to reduce an Indian language to writing: at Kamloops, somewhat later, Father J.M. Le Jeune devised another syllabic script based on Duploye shorthand, in which he printed books and the weekly journal *Kamloops Wawa* in Chinook jargon.

The Catholic priests (and not they alone) were convinced that it was necessary to change the secular as well as spiritual lives of the Indians, and they imposed completely new social and political structures on the communities they converted. In "The Life and Death of an Indian State" (1955), E.M. Lemert has analysed the history of Sechelt and adjacent Coast Salish communities. In 1860, the Sechelt drove away two Oblates who visited them, but two years later they asked for and received a mission, and by 1871 they were all converted. Sechelt was made into a model of "Bishop Durieu's system", a tightly knit community under the control of the priest. Father Durieu, who became Bishop of New Westminster in 1875, initiated the system, and it was put into use wherever circumstances were favourable. At Sechelt, control was put into the hands of four "chiefs" (the recognition of chiefs permitted some carry-over from the native social structure), who had a number of "watchmen" to report on the conduct of the people, and "soldiers" to act as policemen and administer penance or punishment. A "Eucharist chief" assisted the priest in looking after spiritual matters. In the name of temperance, the Indians were required to give up all primitive dances, potlatches, shamanism and gambling, and they were required to participate in the religious forms and rituals of the church. Father Durieu made a point of satisfying the Indians' love of display with church pageantry – large gatherings, processions and passion plays. A most important feature of the system was that the people were moved to a new location where they built a village of modern-style houses and a dominating church. The new order seems to have worked admirably for a time, but by about 1910, as a result of increasing influences from the outside world, the system disintegrated and left (in Lemert's view) a depressed community in its wake.

Of the 40,000 Indians of British Columbia, more than 22,000 are Catholic. A map would show that these are the Indians of most of the area of the province. They include the Carrier, Chilcotin and other Athapaskans (except for a mixture of Anglicans at Telegraph Creek and Atlin); the Kootenay, Shuswap, Okanagan, Lillooet (except for a few Anglicans at Bridge River), Thompson (except those from Lytton to Boston Bar, who are Anglican); most Coast Salish; and the Nootka from Ahousat north to Kyuquot. Catholic residential schools are located at Kuper Island, Mission City, Kamloops, Williams Lake, Lejac, Sechelt, Cranbrook and Lower Post.

Early Protestants
Most of the maritime fur-traders, to be sure, were Protestants, but they were little interested in the salvation of the Indians, and their actions often belied their religion. The first Protestant missionary to visit this part of the world would seem to have been Jonathon S. Green, an American, who accompanied the trading barque *Volunteer* on a voyage to the Northwest Coast in 1829

(Green 1915). He was sent by the American Board of Commissioners for Foreign Missions to investigate the need for a mission on the west coast, and it was largely on the basis of his report that the Oregon Mission was later established. During the summer the ship visited Haida, Tlingit and Tsimshian villages, and Green was able to have long talks with some of the chiefs, who were by then worldly and sophisticated from long association with the traders. But he found a trading ship a poor place in which to teach the virtues of Christianity, as the seamen were obviously failing to practise what he was preaching. He gave religious instruction to a few of the chiefs, deplored the heathenism and sin he saw ashore, and decided that a mission was sorely needed, but he did not return.

Anglicans

It was a British naval captain, J.C. Prevost, who persuaded the Anglicans to enter the mission field on the Northwest Coast. Returning to England in 1856 after a four-year tour on the coast in command of HMS *Virago*, he induced the Church Missionary Society to provide a lay missionary to open a mission at Port Simpson. And the man he took back with him on the newly commissioned HMS *Satellite* was William Duncan. Duncan was the personification of the qualities of missionaries of the time; he had immense faith and courage, and the gigantic audacity required to move uninvited into a large community of foreign and hostile people and single-handedly assume absolute control and reshape their lives. The story of his strong-willed assault on heathenism at Port Simpson, of the establishment of his successful industrial community at Metlakatla, of his bitter and degrading dispute with Bishop Ridley, and of his migration with most of his converts to Alaska to establish New Metlakatla has been told many times (e.g., Wellcome 1887, Arctander 1909, Beynon 1941, Barnett 1942). It might be well to summarize it briefly again, not just because of its innate drama, but because it held the centre of the stage during this period of the history of the coast.

When Duncan arrived in Victoria in 1857, he asked permission from Governor Douglas to go to Port Simpson and live in the fort until he learned the Tsimshian language. Douglas reluctantly agreed, and after a few months in Victoria, Duncan went north on the *Otter*. He found some 2,300 Tsimshian living outside the fort in 140 houses. After eight months spent in learning the language, he ventured forth to preach his first sermon in Tsimshian, repeating it nine times in nine different houses. He found converts, but he also met resistance and hostility. He entered into a continued test of wills with chiefs who saw no reason to give up the established order with its customs and rituals. Year after patient year he preached, and taught school, and held firm to his beliefs, and consolidated his gains. By 1859 he decided that it would be necessary to move his converts and establish a Christian village, and the site he chose was Metlakatla, where the Tsimshian had made their winter homes before they moved to Port Simpson. The move was made in May 1862, just as the first news of the great smallpox epidemic came from Victoria; his converts escaped the disease while heathen Port Simpson suffered severely.

Duncan created at Metlakatla the model of a Christian, self-supporting industrial mission. To live there, people had to conform to 15 laws of conduct, which required them to give up many features of the old life, such as native dances, potlatching, shamanism, gambling, face-painting and alcohol, and also to attend religious instruction, observe the Sabbath, send their children to school, build neat houses, pay the village tax, and be

The solution to Metlakatla's housing problem, 1881. Designed by William Duncan, these uniform houses were made of lumber from the village sawmill. Edward Dossetter photograph, AMNH 42301.

cleanly, industrious, peaceful and honest in trade. In the new social structure all rank and class were abolished, and incredibly (as the Tsimshian had the most elaborate class system on the rank-conscious Northwest Coast) the people conformed. Their energies were absorbed in the new industries that made the village self-supporting. In 1879 Metlakatla made a profound impression on Indian Commissioner Powell when he visited it on his first tour of inspection. He found Duncan presiding over "one of the most orderly, respectable and industrious communities to be found in any Christian country". Its population was about 1,100. In dress, speech and conduct the people were outstanding. Their houses were uniform buildings, 18 by 36 feet (5.5 by 11 metres), with two rooms downstairs and three bedrooms up, and fenced gardens. The church was large enough to seat 800; the school, 500. A sawmill cut all the lumber used in the town, and there was also a sash factory, blacksmith shop, bakery and

William Duncan's church at Metlakatla, 1881. The church seated 800 people and was the dominant building in the model community. Edward Dossetter photograph, AMNH 42293.

weaving house, carpenter shop, and trading post. Plans were being made for a salmon cannery and brick yard (which were later completed). All this was created and controlled by Duncan, and "his individuality seems to me to pervade everything connected with the town" (Powell 1880, p. 114). In a letter to Powell in 1881, Duncan explained the organization of the village. The men were divided (by drawing lots) into ten "companies". Each company had a headman, two elected elders, two constables, three councillors, and ten firemen with a captain. The village tax was three dollars or one week's labour a year (Powell 1882, p. 145).

The dissension that was to divide and destroy this model community began in 1879, when northern British Columbia was made the Diocese of Columbia, and Bishop William Ridley was sent to take charge of Metlakatla and supervise the area. Ridley and Duncan were men of strong character and opposing views; for example, Ridley wanted to introduce at Metlakatla the orthodox ritual of the High Church, but Duncan, a layman, thought it would be misinterpreted by the Indians. The Bishop's high status in the church was matched by Duncan's secure place in the community. The Indians were troubled observers of the interfactional conflict, then took sides and were drawn into it themselves. Ridley had Duncan relieved of his post, and he left for Victoria. An Indian delegation persuaded him to return. Finally he decided that he should move his people once again, and, after a trip to Washington to clear the way, moved in 1887 to Annette Island in Alaska to create a new and even better Metlakatla. Of the 948 people of the community, 823 eventually followed him to Alaska: this was the only large migration of Indians out of British Columbia in historic times. Old Metlakatla lost its industries and its self sufficiency, the old culture enjoyed something of a resurgence, and the influence of the church waned. New Metlakatla was made into an even more modern Christian industrial town, and Duncan reigned there until his death in 1918.

While the history of Metlakatla was unfolding, other Anglican missionaries were at work elsewhere on the northern coast. In 1864, Rev. R.A. Doolan arrived and established a mission on the Nass River near the present Greenville. His place was taken, and the mission moved to Kincolith (to form a Christian village on the model of Metlakatla) in 1867, by Rev. R. Tomlinson. In 1878, Tomlinson went up the Nass and founded the Christian village of Aiyansh, a mission that was the charge after 1883 of Rev. J.B. McCullagh (as described in Moeran 1923). Tomlinson also went to the upper Skeena in 1879 and started a mission north of Kispiox, and later founded an independent mission near Kitwanga. (See Large 1957, pp. 79-84, for a full account of his work and that of his son.)

Rev. W.H. Collison, the author of *In the Wake of the War Canoe* (1915), arrived at Metlakatla in 1873. Three years later he went by canoe to Masset and established a mission among the Haida. His book and another by Rev. Charles Harrison *(Ancient Warriors of the North Pacific,* 1925), who was in charge of the Masset Mission for a time after 1883, are among the best sources of information on the Haida during that time. Collison, in 1880, started another mission up the Skeena River at Hazelton, and later he served for many years at Kincolith. Kisgegas and Kitkatla were other Tsimshian villages where Anglican missions were established.

Down the coast, Rev. A.J. Hall went to Fort Rupert in 1877 (the Catholic mission of St Michael's had just been withdrawn), and two years later moved his mission to Alert Bay. He served there for many years and learned the Kwakiutl language, which enabled him, using a modified alphabet, to print portions of the Bible and prayer books, and to publish a systematic description of the grammar (Hall 1888).

To the north, in 1897, Rev. F.M.T. Palgrave went up the Stikine River to Telegraph Creek and established a mission among the Tahltans. He, too, was something of a scholar, as was his successor, Rev. T.P.W. Thorman, and notes on the Tahltan and their language by these two men are now in the Provincial Archives.

Indians of Anglican faith may be found today on the Queen Charlotte Islands at Masset; on the Nass River at Kincolith, Aiyansh and Greenville (relinquished by the Methodists about 1905); on the Skeena River at Kitwanga and Kitwancool (with a number more at Hazelton and Kitsumkalum); on the coast at Metlakatla, Kitkatla, and the Kwakiutl villages south of Smith Sound and north of Campbell River; in the northern interior mixed among the Tahltan, Atlin and Teslin bands; on the Fraser River from the Lytton band to Boston Bar (with a few more near Ashcroft); and scattered in a few other bands, such as the Squamish. Anglican residential schools are found at Lytton and Alert Bay.

Methodists

By about 1860, Wesleyan Methodist ministers from eastern Canada were at work among both whites and Indians in Victoria and Nanaimo. From these centres, as the need became apparent, they sent out missions to the Indians of outlying areas. Three of the first Methodist ministers to arrive were Revs Ebenezer Robson, Edward White and John B. Good, but probably the principal figure among them was Rev. Thomas Crosby, who described his experiences in two books: *Among the Ankomenums* (1907) and *Up and Down the North Pacific Coast by Canoe and Mission Ship* (1914). The first tells of his early work on the southern coast, and the second tells of his work at Port Simpson and elsewhere up the coast. Crosby arrived in Victoria from Ontario in 1862, and the next year was sent to Nanaimo to start an Indian school and learn the language. His duties took him to all the Coast Salish communities between Victoria and Comox, and also to the Fraser Valley. In 1869 he moved to the Chilliwack Valley and established churches in the vicinity of Sumas and Sardis. His success and that of Rev. C.M. Tate, who followed him to this predominantly Catholic area, culminated in the founding of the Coqualeetza Industrial School (which since 1941 has been used instead as an Indian hospital).

Work on the northern coast grew out of conversions of high-ranking Tsimshian chiefs in a makeshift mission building (converted from a saloon) in Victoria, and their requests for missions in their home villages. Not without some friction with Anglicans already in the field, the Canadian Methodist Missionary Society heeded the call and moved to fill the gaps. In several villages the first steps were taken by native teachers, as told by Rev. W.H. Pierce, himself a converted Tsimshian, in his autobiography *From Potlatch to Pulpit* (1933). The first and most important northern mission was Port Simpson, which had been served only by occasional native preachers since William Duncan moved to Metlakatla in 1862. In 1873 Alfred Dudoward and his wife Kate (both high-ranking Tsimshians who had had white fathers and were educated in Victoria) were converted in Victoria and went home to establish a mission in Port Simpson. Thomas Crosby moved there the following year, and it soon became a Christian community that in some respects rivalled Metlakatla. The church Crosby built seated 1,000 people, and the school and girls' home were also fine buildings.

Visits to other native villages revealed more needs, and Crosby, with the help of native teachers and a small number of ordained missionaries, established several more missions. In 1877, one was started on the Nass River at Lakalzap (later Greenville), near the place where Rev. Doolan had his Anglican mission before moving to Kincolith in 1867. It operated under Rev. A.E. Green and several successors until 1905, when it was relinquished to the Anglicans. Another mission was founded in 1877 at Port Essington, and some years later one was established at Bella Bella, where a boarding school and hospital were later built, and from where the other central coast villages could be reached – Bella Coola, Rivers Inlet and China Hat. The Kitimat Mission was started by a Tsimshian lay teacher named George Edgar, and was served for many years after 1893 by Rev. G.H. Raley. During the 1880s missions were also established up the Skeena River at Kitsegukla and Kispiox, and land was acquired near Hazelton where, in 1900, Dr H.C. Wrinch established the hospital that still bears his name. The call to the Queen Charlotte

Port Simpson, Methodist village, 1884. Thomas Crosby's community rivalled Duncan's Metlakatla in its buildings. Richard Maynard photograph, RBCM PN9320.

Islands came first from a Haida chief of Skidegate named
Gedanst or Amos Russ, who had been converted in Victoria. In
1883, a lay teacher named George Robinson was the first of a suc-
cession of workers to go to Skidegate from Port Simpson, and
soon afterwards, as a result of visits by Rev. Crosby to the more
southerly Haida villages of Tanoo (Clew) and New Gold Harbour, native teachers were sent to these places as well. In 1893,
the Gold Harbour people moved to Skidegate Mission, and in
1897 the Tanoo people, after a ten-year sojourn at New Clew on
Cumshewa Inlet, did the same.

The Presbyterian Church (which in 1925 united with the Meth-
odist and Congregational Churches to form the United Church
of Canada) was active in the mission field on the west coast of
Vancouver Island among the Nootka tribes from Ahousat south.
These tribes are therefore listed in recent statistics with the Methodists under the heading "United Church". Other United
Church Indians live today in the coastal villages of Skidegate,
Port Simpson, Kitamaat, Hartley Bay, Klemtu, Bella Bella, Bella
Coola, Rivers Inlet and Smith Sound; up the Skeena at Kispiox
and Kitsegukla, with some also at Hazelton and Kitwancool; in
the Kwakiutl villages of Cape Mudge and Campbell River; at
Nanaimo, with some in other bands of Vancouver Island Salish;
and in small numbers near Chilliwack in the Fraser Valley. The
residential school at Alberni is administered by the United
Church (Presbyterian).

Salvation Army
Organized on a quasi-military basis in London in 1878 for wide
conquests, the Salvation Army made its presence felt within 10
years in Vancouver and Victoria, and within 20 years among the
Tsimshian on the northern coast and up the Skeena River. Why it
should find such an eager reception among the Tsimshian alone
is difficult to say; perhaps their sudden conversion to staid and
sober Christian lives had left unsatisfied their love of ritual and
display. At any rate, by about 1893, there were signs of rest-
lessness with the church as it was. In a sense, the Salvation Army
cast its shadow before itself. There was no denying that its uniforms, flags and brass bands held a strong attraction for the

Indians. The Anglicans, to keep them within the church, formed the Church Army, patterned on the Salvation Army, and soon all the Anglican mission villages had branches and evangelistic bands (Collison 1915, p. 326). The Methodists met the problem in a similar way, forming branches of the Epworth League within the church.

In Vancouver, Victoria and Seattle, travelling Tsimshians attended meetings of the Army, and their interest became known to the officers of the church. In 1896, Ensign Edgecombe made a trip up the coast to form new detachments, and soon there were branches under native leaders at Port Simpson, Port Essington and Metlakatla (Large 1957, p. 103). A year later a native of Kispiox was converted in Seattle and returned home to hold Army-style meetings throughout the winter. Friction developed between the Salvationists and the Methodists of Kispiox, and in 1898 the new community of Glen Vowell was laid out south of the village. Ensign Thorkalson was sent by the Army to guide the fortunes of the new village, and it has had a white minister ever since. Another group of Salvationists from Kitsegukla settled at

The Salvation Army band at Hazelton, in the early 1900s. St Peter's Church and Mission School are on the left. Morgensen photograph, RBCM PN8407.

Andimaul, south of that village, a short time later, but their settlement did not exist for very many years. Kitselas, downriver at the canyon of the Skeena, also became a Salvation Army village, as did Canyon City on the Nass River. Today, in addition to the places named, there are Salvation Army congregations as minorities at Kincolith, Greenville and Port Simpson.

The Pentecostal Church

The most recent denomination to arrive on the scene, this evangelical movement experienced rapid growth in the cities of the southern parts of the province in the 1920s and 1930s, and has since won considerable followings in many Indian communities, especially those of other Protestant faiths. The coast and upper Skeena villages have felt the impact of this movement in recent years, as have the villages near Victoria and Vancouver.

The Shaker Church

The Indians who became members of the recognized Christian churches did not, in one stroke, discard all their former beliefs about the universe and man's place in it. To one extent or another they reconciled the new teachings with their deeply held beliefs and attitudes from the past. For a generation or so, the beliefs of even the most Christian Indians were actually mixtures of Christian and native thought.

The Shaker Church represents quite another blend of Christian and native beliefs. It is a Christian church and (in Washington State) is officially recognized as such, but its origin is Indian, its congregation is Indian, and its attitudes and rituals have a distinctly Indian flavour. The history of this church has been told in two excellent studies by anthropologists (Gunther 1949, Barnett 1957). It developed in the 1880s in the southern Puget Sound area of Washington, from a prophet cult not unlike those already described. Its founder was John Slocum, an otherwise unremarkable member of the Squaxin tribe. In 1881 or 1882, he "died" and after some hours returned to life. He said that he had reached the gates of heaven but had not been admitted because of his sinful life, and that he had been given the mission of preaching to the Indian people so that they might get to heaven. He asked that a church be built, and before it was completed he began to preach. Some time later he fell seriously ill again. His mourning wife suddenly began to tremble violently as she cared for him, and the shaking seemed to help bring about his cure. It was adopted by members of the church as a supernatural gift of God, and sessions of shaking over sick persons to cure them became one of the main activities of church, and gave it its name.

The church found members to the south in Oregon and to the north as far as Vancouver Island. It reached the Victoria area shortly before 1900, and churches were built at Esquimalt, West Saanich and Duncan. It is still active, although only a small proportion of the Indian people are Shakers. On the mainland the church also has members at Musqueam and North Vancouver. Shaker church buildings are simple and stark, furnished only with a prayer table and benches along the walls. Sunday services include processions with bells and candles, hymn-singing, prayers and brief sermons.

Remnants of Native Religion

The Indians of today consider religion to be synonymous with Christianity, and they are all nominally Christian. Yet a number of beliefs and practices from the old way of life, which were religious in the broader sense of the term (beliefs in supernatural beings and forces, and practices for dealing with them), still persist in some places. The Indians do not consider these part of their religion or see any conflict between them and Christianity.

Old beliefs in spirits, ghosts and other supernatural beings are still held in many areas. An old informant of mine once saw a supernatural monster in the woods (the hairy giant or Sasquatch) and fell unconscious from the shock; another had a finger permanently numbed from touching a ghost while he was attempting to brush it out of the house with a flaming paper torch; and a third always fasted and bathed before going out in his fish boat, so that the salmon spirits would be pleased and favour him. The treatment of some kinds of illnesses by shamans or Indian doctors is still quietly practised in some areas. This is especially true where spirit dancing is still carried on: a dancer's "power" sometimes becomes blocked in his chest so that he is unable to sing its song properly, and the manipulations of a shaman are required to put it right. One suspects that in some places a fear of witchcraft still lingers beneath the surface (see Honigmann 1947).

In former times the most prominent religious ceremonies of the Indians were the winter dances, though in fact these were partly religious ritual and partly secular stagecraft. The elaborate masked dances of the Kwakiutl and northern tribes were mostly stagecraft; few of the people believed that the dancers were really imbued with supernatural power, or that the masked figures were actually supernatural creatures. The fragments that have survived are purely stagecraft; their religious significance exists only in dimming memories. In sharp contrast, the Coast Salish spirit dances were intensely religious in nature, since each dancer had his own individual guardian spirit that possessed him during the dance. Some of the religious meaning has been lost as Indian life has changed, but spirit dancing is still practised by many Coast Salish (and in a somewhat different form by some Interior Salish) and still provides them with experiences that are in the broad sense religious.

Spirit dancers are found among the Coast Salish tribes from Nanaimo to Victoria on Vancouver Island, and from North Vancouver to northern Puget Sound on the mainland. Initiation as a new dancer, which usually occurs in the late teens, still involves the acquisition of a supernatural power. In some cases the power has entered the individual earlier in life (it may cause a sickness that can only be cured by initiation as a dancer), but more often nowadays it is breathed into him (or her) by the older dancers, who begin the initiation by going through the motions of forcibly abducting the unsuspecting initiate. The power brings with it distinctive personal variations in the song, dance, costume and pattern of painting the face. For four days, while these are being learned, the new dancer undergoes special rituals and observances to help him through this important period of change in his life, and for the remainder of the dancing season he is expected to live in the dance house, wear a special costume, and observe certain other restrictions.

The dance houses are large barnlike structures with dirt floors and tiers of benches around the walls, heated by two large bonfires. On reserves where there are new dancers, dances are held almost every night of the season, attended by the local people only. In addition, almost every week-end from mid January to mid April a large spirit dance is held in one or other of the villages, attended by up to 1,000 people from all over the area. These are used also as occasions for many of the social ceremonies formerly performed at potlatches, such as the conferring of Indian names, the honouring of dead members of the family, and the display of special family-owned rituals and dances. The spirit dancing may not begin until well after midnight, and may continue well into the following forenoon. Upwards of a hundred dancers may perform. One at a time in their turn, the dancers become possessed, rise, dance clockwise around the house and are assisted back to their seats. The spectators help by drumming and singing the dancer's song. The dance costumes, especially those of the men, are often spectacular, with long pointed headdresses of human hair surmounted by swivelled pairs of eagle feathers, and black velvet shirts and trousers decorated with rows of sequins and small paddles (cf. Suttles 1963, pp. 517-518 and 519-521).

There is little indication that spirit dancing will die out within the near future; on the contrary, it gives the impression of being a flourishing and still-evolving activity. Anthropologists have been much interested in the reasons for its persistence, and have concluded that it provides the dancers with strong satisfaction, even in today's world. The spirit dancer experiences profound sensations that are fundamentally religious in nature; furthermore, he has the social security that comes from belonging to an exclusive group, he has an emotional safety valve that provides a release of tensions in a socially approved way and he has discovered a method of asserting his identity as an Indian.

Somewhat the same reasons probably explain the persistence, on southern Vancouver Island around Victoria, of another winter ceremony locally known as the Black-face Dance. This is a secret society derived from the Nootka Wolf ritual, which diffused to the Salish tribes bordering Juan de Fuca Strait (Ernst 1952; Gunther 1927, pp. 281-288), but it is clothed in more secrecy now than it ever was in the past. Membership is restricted to certain family lines, and the meetings are so exclusive that members may not even take their spouses. On rare occasions the group performs in public at a spirit dance, and shows dances using wolf masks and bird rattles, and complex tableaus of large human and animal figures with movable parts.

Social Disorganization

Social rules and usages are those that define who our relatives are and control the ways in which we get along with other people in our society, relatives and non-relatives. The Indians, especially those of the coast tribes, had rich and elaborate patterns of social organization. In the virtual absence of political institutions they regulated their lives by social institutions. Their social structures were built on two basic themes – kinship and rank – both of which were more important in their society than in ours. Kinship ties were defined in a number of different ways, but they were always recognized among distant as well as close relatives. Inheritance along these lines of kinship determined how a person was to conduct his life: what social class he belonged to, what positions of rank he could attain, where he could live, whom he could marry, where he could hunt and fish, what crests he could use, and so on. Men were not all born equal: there was social stratification into classes (nobility, commoners and slaves), and in each tribe there was a graded series of positions of rank. The rules brought by the white man conflicted with most of these old usages, which as a result have been discarded as obsolete. One feels that in this aspect of culture, perhaps more than in others, the Indians have given up more than they have received in return.

Much of the old social organization was demolished under the frontal attack of the church. When the missionaries swept out heathenism, they included the social forms that supported it – potlatches, winter dances, and the systems of class and rank. Duncan at Metlakatla stamped these out completely for a while, and Bishop Durieu's system for Catholic communities did much the same thing. But potlatching and winter dancing did not die easily; in fact, the main effect of early white contacts was to stimulate them to greater vigour. For many years the missionaries and Indian agents saw potlatching and winter dancing as evil, and suppressed them with the Indian Act. The long and unsuccessful attempt to stamp out Kwakiutl potlatching by law has been described by La Violette (1961), Codere (1950) and Halliday (1935). Slavery passed out of the picture without a struggle in the 1860s. The same applies to warfare, and the custom of avenging one murder by committing another. British law and order were not enforced until the 1850s (except when a white man was involved), and by that time a few object lessons were sufficient to make the Indians conform. Other customs were discouraged by the whites for no better reason than that they somehow didn't seem proper; for example, the disposal of the dead by cremation or in burial houses or caves, and descent of names and property in the maternal line. Marriages arranged to form alliances between social groups, and accompanied by exchange of gifts, looked to the whites like a violation of the right of individuals to choose their own mates, and like the sale of brides.

A great body of social custom passed from the scene because it had become obsolete in the new circumstances. The new laws about ownership and descent of property removed much of the reason for existence of the kinship groups and the old rules of descent. New ideas about marriage have caused the strict law of exogamy to be discarded. Hereditary chieftainship still brings respect, but no longer carries its former power; some bands still choose their chiefs by band custom, but more often now the hereditary chiefs take a back seat to the elected chiefs and councillors. With the passing of potlatches and winter ceremonies went the oratory, songs, dances and costumes that formed a part of them. Masks and other paraphernalia were no longer needed. With crests out of fashion, there was no more reason for making totem poles. The young and modern Indians regarded these things as old fashioned.

Names

The English system of assigning personal names is very different from the old Indian systems, and a brief description of the transition from the old to the new will serve as a revealing example of the ways in which individuals have been affected by the forces of change. Names do more than just identify individuals, they also give some indication of their places in the social structure. Our own names reveal our sex and father's line, and sometimes our marital status (Mrs), educational attainment (Ph.D.), occupation (Mr Justice) or military rank (Col). On the northern coast, Indian individuals took a series of names of higher and higher rank as they grew older, and each one usually revealed to other members of the tribe the person's sex, age-group, lineage, rank and sometimes role (such as successor to the chief). To the extent that the old social structure still survives, Indian names are still used and show the statuses of individuals within it.

The adoption of the English language and British law made it necessary for the Indians to adopt English names. Partly it was a matter of convenience, for the whites could not pronounce, let alone write, most Indian names. Sometimes a man was given a first name; for example, Tom. This would then become the surname of his children; for example, Sam Tom or Lizzie Tom (which might become Samuel Thomas and Elizabeth Thomas). Grandchildren usually kept the same surname (Jack Tom), but in some cases they chose to continue the custom of using the father's first name (Jack Sam). In this way, many Indian families came to have English first names as their surnames. It was another common practice to take the name of the missionary or other patron at the time of baptism, which may account for the Whites and Goods at Nanaimo and the Collisons at Skidegate, or to take the name of some famous person, as did old Chief Edenshaw of Masset when he was baptized Albert Edward Edenshaw after the British king. In some cases the Indian name was translated into English and used as a surname: *Maquilla* of Salmon River became Johnny Moon; a well-known Aiyansh man whose boyhood name may be translated "in-spring(water)-bright-where-sits-the-frog" (frog sitting in a spring of water illuminated by a shaft of sunlight) took the name Michael Inspring

Bright. In other cases the Indian name sounded somewhat similar to an English surname, and the anglicized spelling was adopted: at Alert Bay *Walas* ("great") became Wallace; at Kitsegukla, *Guksan* became Cookson. Often the Indian name itself, somewhat simplified, could be used, as, for example, Clutesi, Siwid, Muldo, Neeselowes. Complications arose in tribes where Indian names were passed down in the maternal line: an Indian name adopted as a surname passed from a man to his own children, who were not members of his clan and had no right to the name. At Hazelton, for example, the name Muldo (a simplification of *Gitemguldo*) belongs to the Frog clan and is passed on within the clan in the maternal line. At the same time it has come to be used as a surname, and is passed in the male line to people who are members of other clans.

Most Indian families still confer Indian names on their children. These are used mainly on ceremonial occasions when the old social structure is in force, and they place a certain obligation on their bearers to take an interest in the old cultures.

Survivals

The modern life of many Indian groups is still flavoured with traces of the old social customs. Some villages still have frequent gatherings and feasts where echoes of past oratory and formality are heard, and old costumes and crests are sometimes seen. Some families still remember clan traditions; in fact, there is now a revival of pride in such things among the people of the Skeena and Nass rivers. Most Indians still show a greater awareness of kinship ties than whites are in the habit of doing, and they maintain their contacts with distant relatives. Modern transportation and communications, which permit easier and more frequent contact among relatives, have strengthened the inter-village ties in the Coast Salish area (see Suttles 1963). In this area the individual village never was a self-sufficient social unit. The whole area was bound together by a web of social ties, and in a sense the whole area was a community. Modern conditions have strengthened the ties of this community. This is seen in the spirit dance gatherings during the winter and the canoe races of the early summer, which bring together large numbers of Coast

Salish people. Spirit dances have already been briefly described. These are occasions for much speech-making in the Indian languages, and the speeches make constant reference to the ties of kinship that hold the people together, and exhort the young to respect the memories of the ancestors who were the previous owners of their honoured names, and to maintain the old traditions (Suttles 1963, p. 519). The canoe races, which are attended by non-Indians as well, have some of the aspects of modern festivals – drill teams, sports contests, modern dances, barbecues and the crowning of princesses. But these gatherings also have some of the feeling of old-time potlatches, and in the speeches the same themes are emphasized as at the spirit dances. The Indian pow-wows held in recent years at North Vancouver, the Indian Days at Kamloops, and other gatherings, such as the Williams Lake stampedes, are similar occasions for Indians to enjoy renewed social contacts and gain recognition as Indians. They might be considered examples of neo-Indian culture.

One factor that contributes to the persistence and growth of these neo-Indian activities is the social barrier that still discourages many of these people from entering fully into the social life of the communities surrounding them. In places, this barrier is being breached by the activities of joint Parent-Teacher Associations, Boy Scouts, YMCA, YWCA and clubs such as the Mika Nika Club of Kamloops, and the establishment of friendship houses in the larger cities. On the national level, an increased appreciation of Indian contributions to the culture of the country was shown by the presentation of a Canada Council medal to the late Mungo Martin in 1963. Yet any impartial observer can see that some degree of prejudice still operates to segregate the Indians socially. On their part, many Indians still harbour a deep sense of grievance, which has been called a "heritage of bitterness". The social gap is still wide.

New Forms of Political Organization

To exercise control over matters that affect them as a group, the people of an area usually establish some form of governing organization to which they delegate the necessary authority. The Indians of our region, however, had little in the way of such political institutions. They preferred to govern their affairs more as groups of kinfolk spread over wide areas than as local groups sharing the occupancy of defined territories. Political organization, that is to say, took second place to social organization. A man's influence depended upon his social status, and his power as a leader grew out of the obligations owed to him through kinship and marriage. The local tribes were composed of more or less uneasy alliances of such kin-groups; no effective form of organization was developed above the level of the tribe; and, of course, nothing comparable to a state or kingdom ever evolved.

The adaptation of the Indians to modern Canadian society may be measured in terms of their success in adopting political institutions to govern their local affairs and to gain some measure of control over issues that affect Indians as a whole. On the local level, as we have seen, there were a number of attempts by missionaries to impose completely new structures, and some of these met with notable but temporary success. Later the government imposed a system of organization into bands and agencies, which largely took its form from the old pattern of political organization (or lack of it), but involved new techniques for governing that the Indians had to learn. In the church-imposed systems the real power had remained in the hands of the missionary; in the government-imposed system the power remains in the hands of the Indian Superintendent. On the intertribal level there has been a growth of Indian organizations whose purpose is to speak for the Indians on regional and national issues. On the even higher level of provincial and federal politics, the Indians are beginning to take an active role as voters and even occasionally as candidates, though they find themselves to be only a small and ineffective minority in those larger arenas.

The band system of local administration grew out of the atomistic nature of the aboriginal political system. In its dealings with the native people the government could find no effective groups to work with larger than the local tribes or bands, and these local groups have remained as the basic units of organization. Officially, Indians are not simply Indians; they are registered members of one or other of the 189 bands in the province. Lands, funds, problems of administration and projects of community development are all usually handled at the level of the band. The band councils do provide a training ground in which a large number of individuals are learning the techniques of governing, and Indians are being encouraged to assume increasing control over local affairs. But, as has already been pointed out, the band is usually too small a unit to be effective in today's conditions. The Indian Affairs Branch has recognized the need for larger groupings in two ways: first, they have attempted to amalgamate small bands with larger ones; and, second, they are attempting to establish agency councils. The latter type of organization, made up of representation from all the bands in each agency, will likely play a more important role in future.

British Columbia Indians have shown considerable initiative in forming intertribal organizations or brotherhoods, and these have had a significant effect on the conduct of Indian administration in Canada. The formation of the Nishga Land Committee in 1913 and of the Allied Tribes of British Columbia in 1916 has already been described. The issue about which they rallied at that time was the Land Question, and when that matter was declared closed by the Senate-House Committee in 1927, the Allied Tribes dissolved. But there were other questions of common concern to all the Indians: the Indian Act, the place of the Indian in the fishing industry, hunting and fishing rights, and the Land Question, which was not really a dead issue. New organizations soon began to appear on the scene.

The first of these was the Native Brotherhood of British Columbia. In 1931, the late Alfred Adams of Masset, who was familiar with the organization of the Alaska Native Brotherhood, discussed with William Beynon and other Tsimshian chiefs the possibility of forming a similar intertribal organization in British Columbia. Delegations from Masset and the Coast Tsimshian villages met that winter in Port Simpson, and the Brotherhood was formed. Through the 1930s it continued to meet annually at Port Simpson, and it increased its membership by the establishment of branches in other Tsimshian and Northern Kwakiutl villages. In 1936, the Southern Kwakiutl formed a labour union known as the Pacific Coast Native Fishermen's Association, and in 1942 this group joined the Brotherhood, and a business office was opened in Vancouver. From that time on the centre of the organization has been Vancouver, and one of its main functions has been to serve as a union for coastal Indian fishermen. New branches were formed on the coast north of Cape Mudge and at several villages in the interior. In 1946 the Brotherhood started its own monthly newspaper, *The Native Voice**, which has effectively presented Indian views ever since. When hearings were opened in Ottawa on the revision of the Indian Act in 1947, the Brotherhood was invited to send delegates, and their voices helped to frame the improvements embodied in the new Act of 1951. Annual meetings continue to be held at centres throughout the province, and the Native Brotherhood continues to be an active and important force in Indian affairs. (See Drucker 1958 for a study of this organization and its Alaskan counterpart.)

A second such intertribal organization, the North American Indian Brotherhood, was started in 1945 as an offshoot of the Native Brotherhood. Andrew Paull, one of the strong leaders of the latter group, broke off and took the Coast Salish and Nootka branches with him into the new organization. It has gained additional strength by the addition of Interior Salish branches, and has ties with other Indian organizations outside the province.

In 1955, the Nishga Tribal Council was formed, to replace the old Nishga Land Committee, with branches in the four Nass River villages of Kincolith, Greenville, Canyon City and Aiyansh. Its purpose is to work in general for Indian welfare, and it continues to press for a settlement of the Land Question as set out in the Nishga Petition of 1913. With the recent resurgence of interest in that issue, the Nishga Tribal Council and the two broth-

---

* Note for the new edition: *The Native Voice* is published by the Native Brotherhood; its mailing address is 415B West Esplanade, North Vancouver, V7M 1A6.

erhoods have taken preliminary steps to unite for the purpose of presenting their case before the proposed Indian Claims Commission. On Vancouver Island two additional intertribal organizations have recently been formed, one among the Nootka and the other among the Coast Salish. Whether these will be permanent and effective bodies remains to be seen.

The Indians will undoubtedly remain a distinct ethnic group for many generations to come, living for the most part in separate communities with somewhat different ways of life stemming from their distinct racial background, history and cultural heritage. There seems no reason why they should not attain equality in educational standards, occupations, and social life, and gain complete control over their own affairs. Their lives have changed drastically during the past century, and will have to change more, but they should always retain the right to find their own identity and develop their own lives as they wish within the framework of Canadian society.

This unverified photograph is probably of a Salvation Army band in Coast Tsimshian territory. Note the "Blood and Fire" slogan on the flag. Photo: R.T. Tashiro. RBCM PN4795

Appendix 1:
Phonemes and Phonetic Key

The sounds used in human languages are produced by forcing a column of air through the vocal apparatus and modifying its passage by vibrating the vocal cords and by varying the positions of the throat, tongue and lips. Broadly speaking, the sounds are of two main types: consonants, which are produced by temporarily stopping or partially restricting the passage of air, and vowels, made by passing the air unobstructed through the mouth.

Consonants produced by closing the air passage completely are called stops. In English we have three pairs of stops – *p* and *b*, *t* and *d*, *k* and *g*. Sounds produced by forcing the air through a partially obstructed passage are usually called fricatives, and are quite common in English – *f*, *v*, *θ* (the *th* in "thing"), *δ* (the *th* in "this"), *s*, *z*, *š* (the *sh* in "show"), *ž* (the *z* in "azure") and *h*. An affricative is a combination of a stop with its related fricative, as in the English examples *č* (the *ch* in "church") and *ǰ* (the *dge* in "judge"). To produce other consonant sounds usually known as continuants, the passage of air is modified in various different ways. The nasals, *m*, *n* and *ŋ* (the *ng* in "singer"), channel it through the nose; the laterals (*l* sounds), around the tongue. With the semivowels (*y*, *w*), there is almost no obstruction.

Consonants may be pronounced either with or without vibrations of the vocal cords; that is, they may be either voiced (sonants) or unvoiced (surds). The difference may be heard by pronouncing the pairs *b* and *p*, *g* and *k*, *d* and *t*, *s* and *z*, which are the same sounds except for this voicing. Consonants may also be glottalized; that is, made more intense and explosive by closing the glottis (vocal cords) and then releasing the tension suddenly as the sound is pronounced. In the Indian languages it is common to find the stops, affricatives and continuants glottalized to form additional series of phonemes.

The consonant sound is affected not just by the degree of closure, but also by the place in the vocal apparatus where closure occurs. If the obstruction is formed by the lips (bilabial closure), the stops are *p* and *b*, and the corresponding nasal is *m*. Interdental closure produces θ and δ (*th*); an alveolar constriction (tongue tip against the ridge behind the upper teeth) produces *t, d, n, s, z, c (ts)*, ʒ (*dz*), *č (ch)* and ǰ (*dge*). If the constriction is palatal (mid tongue against soft palate), the guttural sounds *k, g, and* η (*ng*) are formed. The constriction may occur even farther back: velar (base of tongue against uvula) or glottal (in the vocal cords themselves); but except for the doubtful case of *h*, we have no examples of the latter in English.

The different vowel sounds are produced by altering the positions of the tongue and lips to change the shape of the vocal chamber through which the air is passing. In this way a whole continuum of sounds may be produced. Our alphabet fails to distinguish clearly even the sounds used in English, which include *i* (as in "m*ee*t"), ι ("p*i*t"), *e* ("l*a*te"), ε ("p*e*t"), *ȧ* ("p*a*t"), *a* ("f*a*ther"), α ("n*u*t"), ɔ ("l*aw*"), *o* ("m*o*le"), *u* ("b*oo*t"), ə ("*a*gain").

Diphthongs are combinations of vowels; for example, *oi* (as in "*oi*l"), *aw* ("h*ou*se"), *ay* ("h*igh*"), *ey* ("pl*ay*") and *ow* ("sh*ow*").

PHONETIC KEY

There follows a list of phonemes used in British Columbia
Indian languages (of course no single language uses them all). A
professional linguist would refine this list by making further
distinctions between similar sounds, but this list is complete
enough for the degree of precision we desire.

CONSONANTS

Stops
p b t d k g – as in English (intermediates B D G may be present
   instead of sonants *b d g*).
q g – farther back than *k* and *g*.
k˙ g˙ (kʸ gʸ) – farther forward than *k* and *g*, adding a *y* sound, as
   in "than*k y*ou".
kʷ gʷ qʷ, gʷ – labialized, as in "*qu*ince", "*Gw*en", etc.
p′ t′ k′ q′ k˙′ k′ʷ g′ʷ – glottalized (formerly written *p!*, *t!*, etc.).
ʔ – the glottal stop, as in "Hawai*ʔ*i".

Fricatives
θ – as in "*th*ing".
s z – same as English phonemes.
š – as in "*sh*ow".
ž – as in "a*z*ure".
ł – surd *l*, as in "a*thl*ete", whispered and slurred into a single
   sound with tongue in the *l* position.
x – as in German "i*ch*".
x̣ – as in Scottish "lo*ch*".
γ – sonant form of *x*, a gargle-like sound.
γ̣ – sonant form of *x̣*, like French *r* in "Paris".
x˙ γ˙ – palatalized *x* (farther forward).
xʷ x̣ʷ γʷ γ̣ʷ – labialized (lips rounded).
h – same as English phoneme.

Affricatives

ç – *t* plus *θ*, as in "eigh*th*".
c – *t* plus *s*, as in "ca*ts*".
č – as in "*ch*ur*ch*".
ʒ – as in "a*dz*e".
ǰ – as in "*judge*".
λ – *dl*.
ƛ – *t* plus *ɬ*.
ç′ c′ č′ ƛ′ – glottalized.

Continuants

m n y l w – same as English phonemes.
m′ n′ y′ l′ w′ – glottalized.
η – as in "si*n*ger".

Vowels

i – as in "s*ee*k".
ɪ – as in "p*i*t".
e – as in "l*a*te".
ε – as in "p*e*t".
à – as in "c*a*t".
a – as in "f*a*ther".
α – as in "b*u*t".
ə – as in "*a*gain".
o – as in "m*o*le".
ɔ – as in "l*aw*".
u – as in "b*oo*t".

In any given language this range is divided into perhaps five or six phonemic vowels.

ACCENT OR STRESS

It is extremely important to place stress on the proper syllables. The accent (ʹ) is placed after the vowel of the stressed syllable, as in čɪlkoʹtən (Chilcotin), xayʹdə (Haida).

LENGTH

Phonemes marked with a dot *(aˑ, 1ˑ, mˑ)* are sounded for double the normal length of time.

MARIUS BARBEAU'S PHONETIC SYSTEM

Since so many of the books on British Columbia Indian subjects were written by Dr Marius Barbeau, using his unique style of transcription of Indian names, it might be helpful to compare his system with this one. Briefly, he has attempted to use the English alphabet to transcribe Indian sounds; for example, his *ae* is the sound ɛ, his *aw* is ɔ, his *r* is γ and often χ, his *rh* is x or χ, his *hl* is ɬ, his *gy* is gʹ. He uses the phonemic glottal stop freely, as in *taʔawdzep.* We may give a few examples of the same name in his system and in ours:

Gitrhahla	gʹɪtxaʹɬa	(Kitkatla)
Legyarh	legɛʹx	(Legaic)
Gitrhawn	gʹɪtxɔn	(Gitkun)
Rhaida	xayʹdə	(Haida)

Appendix 2:
First Nations' Names in the 1990s

The table on the facing page equates the names used in this book with the commonly accepted names in use today. The modern names are used on the maps following on page 166 and 167. The pronunciations are general approximations, because there are differences in the way individual First Peoples say these names. For ease of use we have used the regular alphabet in the pronunciation guide, rather than the linguistic symbols described in Appendix 1; but note that the italic *x* designates the fricative phoneme, as in the German *"ich"*.

Important note:
Recent treaty negotiations have resulted in First Nations redefining themselves and their territories. Consequently, the actual names and territiories of First Nations may differ from those in Wilson Duff's maps and from the new maps and table shown here.

Table 5. First Nations Names, 1997.

1965 Name	Modern Name	Pronunciation
Athapaskan	Athapaskan	Ath-a-pass-kan
Beaver	Dunne-za	De-nay-za
Bella Coola	Nuxalk	New-halk
Carrier	Carrier (Dakelh)	(Da-kelh)
Chilcotin	Tsilhqot'in	Tsil-ko-teen
Comox	Comox	Koe-moks
Gitksan	Gitxsan	Git-ksan
Haida	Haida	Hydah
Haisla	Haisla	Hyzlah
Halkomelem	Halkomelem	Halk-o-may-lem
Heiltsuk	Heiltsuk	Hel-tsuk
Kaska	Kaska	Kas-ka
Kootenay	Ktunaxa	Doon-ah-hah
Kwakiutl, Southern	Kwakwaka'wakw	Kwak-wak-ee-wakw
Kwakiutl, Northern	Oweekeno	O-wik-en-o
Lillooet	Stl'atl'imx	Stlat-liemx
Niska (Nishga)	Nisga'a	Nis-gaa
Nootka	Nuu-chah-nulth	New-chah-nulth
Okanagan	Okanagan	O-kan-a-gan
Salish	Salish	Say-lish
Sechelt	Sechelt	See-shelt
Sekani	Sekani	Sik-an-ee
Shuswap	Secwepemc	Se-wep-mx
Slave	Dene-thah	De-nay-ta
Squamish	Squamish	Skwamish
Tahltan	Tahltan	Tall-ten
Thompson	Nlaka'pamux	Ng-khla-kap-muhx
Tlingit	Tlingit	Tling-git
Tsimshian	Tsimshian	Sim-she-an

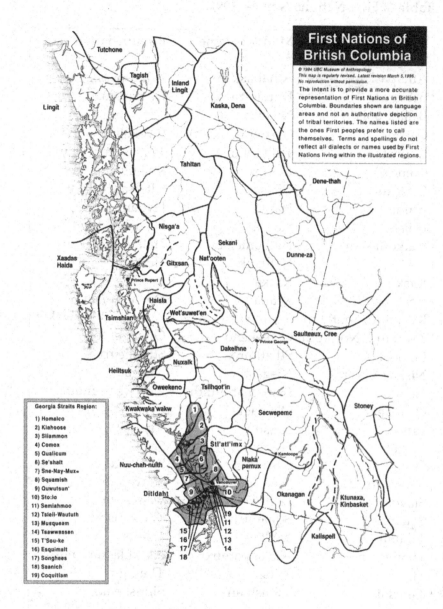

Map 6: First Nations of British Columbia, 1996.

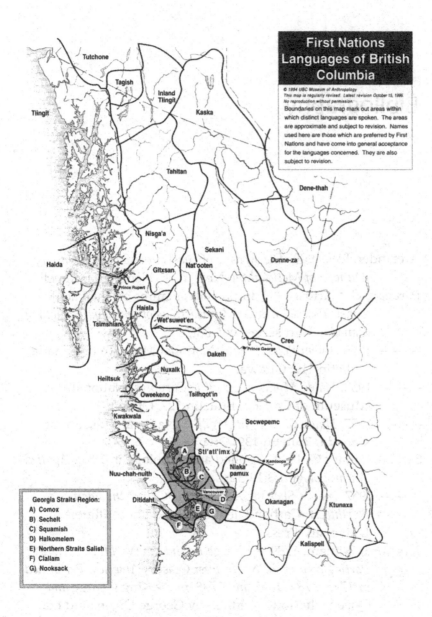

Map 7: First Nations Languages of British Columbia, 1996.

Bibliography

Arctander, J.W. 1909. *The Apostle of Alaska: the Story of William Duncan of Metlakahtla*. New York: Fleming H. Revell.

Barbeau, C. Marius. 1939. Indian silversmiths on the Pacific coast. *Proceedings and Transactions of the Royal Society of Canada*, third series, vol. 33:2.

———. 1950. *Totem Poles*. 2 vols. National Museum of Canada, Bulletin 119. Ottawa.

———. 1953. *Haida Myths in Argillite Carvings*. National Museum of Canada, Bulletin 127. Ottawa.

———. 1957. *Haida Carvers in Argillite*. National Museum of Canada, Bulletin 139. Ottawa.

Barnett, Homer G. 1942. Applied anthropology in 1860. *Applied Anthropology* 1:3:19-32.

———. 1957. *Indian Shakers: A Messianic Cult of the Pacific Northwest*. Carbondale, Illinois: Southern Illinois University Press.

Beresford, William. 1789. *A Voyage Round the World; But More Particularly to the North-west Coast of America: Performed in 1785, 1786, 1787 and 1788, in the King George and Queen Charlotte...*, edited by George Dixon. 2nd ed. London: Geo. Goulding. [Reprint, 1968, in: *Biblioteca Australiana* no. 37. New York: Da Capo Press.]

Beynon, William. 1941. The Tsimshians of Metlakatla, Alaska. *American Anthropologist*, 43:83-88.

Bishop, Charles. 1794-96. Journal of the ship, *Ruby*. Typescript copy in the Provincial Archives, Victoria.

British Columbia. 1875. Lands and Works Department. *Papers connected with the Indian Land Question, 1850-75.* Victoria.

————. 1888. *Papers relating to the Commission Appointed to Enquire into the Conditions of the Indians of the North-west Coast.* Victoria.

————. 1916. *Report of the Royal Commission on Indian Affairs for the Province of British Columbia,* 4 volumes. Victoria.

————. 1950-63. Department of the Provincial Secretary, Indian Advisory Committee. Annual Reports. Victoria.

————. 1963. Department of Health Services *Vital Statistics of the Province of British Columbia.* Victoria.

British Columbia Natural Resources Conference. 1956. *British Columbia Atlas of Resources.* Victoria.

Cail, Robert E. 1956. Disposal of Crown lands in British Columbia, 1871-1913. Master's thesis, Department of History, University of British Columbia, Vancouver.

Canada. 1872-79. Annual Reports of the Deputy Superintendent General of Indian Affairs. Ottawa.

————. 1880-1916. Department of Indian Affairs. Annual Reports. Ottawa.

————. 1913. Handbook of Indians of Canada. Sessional Paper no. 21a. Appendix to the *Tenth Report of the Geographic Board of Canada.* Ottawa.

————. 1927. Report and evidence, Special Joint Committee on Claims of the Allied Indian Tribes. Ottawa.

————. 1959. Department of Citizenship and Immigration, Indian Affairs Branch. *The Canadian Indian: A Reference Paper.* Ottawa.

————. 1960. Indian Affairs Branch. *Indians of British Columbia (An Historical Review).* Ottawa.

————. 1962-63. Annual Reports. Ottawa.

Codere, Helen. 1950. *Fighting With Property: A Study of Kwakiutl Potlatching and Warfare, 1792-1930.* Monographs of the American Ethnological Society 18. New York: J.J. Augustin.

Collison, W.H. 1915. *In the Wake of the War Canoe*. London: n.p.

Cook, S.F. 1955. The Epidemic of 1830-1833 in California and Oregon. *University of California Publications in American Archaeology and Ethnology* 43:3.

Crosby, Thomas. 1907. *Among the An-ko-me nums*. Toronto: William Briggs.

———. 1914. *Up and Down the North Pacific Coast by Canoe and Mission Ship*. Toronto: The Missionary Society of the Methodist Church, the Young Peoples' Forward Movement Department.

Denver Art Museum. n.d. Indian Leaflet Series. Denver, Colorado: Denver Art Museum.

Douglas, James. 1874. Letter to Lt-Col Powell, Indian Commissioner. Provincial Archives, Victoria.

Drucker, Philip. 1958. *The Native Brotherhoods: Modern Intertribal Organizations on the Northwest Coast*. U.S. Bureau of American Ethnology, Bulletin 168, Washington, D.C.

Duff, Wilson. 1952a. *The Upper Stalo Indians*. Anthropology in British Columbia Memoir No. 1. Victoria: British Columbia Provincial Museum.

———. 1952b. *Anthropology in British Columbia*, No. 3: *Gitksan Totem Poles, 1952*. Victoria: British Columbia Provincial Museum.

———. 1959. *Histories, Territories and Laws of the Kitwancool*. Anthropology in British Columbia Memoir No. 4. Reprint, 1989. Victoria: Royal British Columbia Museum.

———. 1963. *Thunderbird Park*. Victoria: British Columbia Government Travel Bureau.

———. 1964. Contributions of Marius Barbeau to west-coast ethnology. *Anthropologica* (New Series) 6:1.

Duff, Wilson, and Michael Kew. 1958. Anthony Island, a home of the Haidas. In *Provincial Museum Report for the Year 1957*. Victoria: Province of British Columbia, Department of Education.

Dunn, John. 1845. History of the Oregon Territory and the British North American fur-trade. *Smith's Weekly* (Philadelphia).

Ernst, Alice H. 1952. *The Wolf Ritual of the Northwest Coast.*
    Eugene: University of Oregon Press.
Ford, C.S. 1941. *Smoke from Their Fires: the Life of a Kwakiutl*
    Chief. New Haven, Conn.: Yale University Press.
Gladstone, Percy. 1953. Native Indians and the fishing industry
    of British Columbia. *Canadian Journal of Economics and*
    Political Science, vol. 19, pp. 20-34.
Green, J.S. 1915. *Journal of a Tour on the Northwest Coast of*
    America in the Year 1829. Hartman's Historical Series
    10. New York: C.F. Hartman.
Gunther, Erna. 1927. *Klallam Ethnography.* Seattle: University of
    Washington Press.
————. 1949. The Shaker religion of the northwest. In *Indians of*
    the Urban Northwest, edited by M.W. Smith. New York:
    Columbia University Press.
————. 1962. *Northwest Coast Indian Art: an Exhibit at the Seattle*
    World's Fair Fine Arts Pavilion. Seattle: n.p.
Haeberlin, H.K., James A. Teit and Helen H. Roberts. 1928.
    Coiled basketry in British Columbia and surrounding
    region. In U.S. Bureau of American Ethnology *41st*
    Annual Report. Washington, D.C.
Hall, A.J. 1888. A grammar of the Kwagiutl language. In
    Transactions of the Royal Society of Canada 6:2.
Halliday, W.M. 1935. *Potlatch and Totem, and The Recollections of*
    an Indian Agent. Toronto: J.M. Dent and Sons.
Harrison, C. 1925. *Ancient Warriors of the North Pacific: The*
    Haidas, Their Laws, Customs and Legends with some
    Historical Account of the Queen Charlotte Islands.
    London: H.F. and G. Witherby.
Hawthorn, H.B., C.S. Belshaw and S.M. Jamieson. 1958. *The*
    Indians of British Columbia: A Study of Contemporary
    Social Adjustment. Toronto: University of Toronto
    Press; Vancouver: University of British Columbia
    Press.
Heizer, R.F. 1941. The introduction of Monterey shells to the
    Indians of the Northwest Coast. *Pacific Northwest*
    Quarterly 31:399-402.
Hill-Tout, Charles. 1907. *British North America,* 1: *The Far West:*

The Home of the Salish and Dene. London: Archibald
Constable.

Honigmann, J.J. 1947. Witch-fear in post-contact Kaska society.
American Anthropologist 49:222-43.

Howay, F.W. 1941. The first use of sail by the Indians of the
Northwest Coast. *American Neptune* 1:374-80.

———. 1942. The introduction of intoxicating liquors amongst
the Indians of the Northwest Coast. *British Columbia
Historical Quarterly,* vol. 6.

Jamieson, S., and Percy Gladstone. 1950. Unionism in the
fishing industry of British Columbia. *Canadian Journal
of Economics and Political Science,* February 1950, pp. 1-
11; May 1950. pp. 146-71.

Jenness, D. 1943. *The Carrier Indians of the Bulkley River: Their
Social and Religious Life.* U.S. Bureau of American
Ethnology, Bulletin 133, Washington, D.C.

Keithahn, E.L. 1963. *Monuments in Cedar.* Seattle: Superior
Publishing Co.

Krause, Aurel. 1956. *The Tlingit Indians: Results of a Trip to the
Northwest Coast of America and Bering Straits,* translated
by Erna Gunther. Monographs of the American
Ethnological Society 26. Seattle: University of
Washington Press.

Kroeber, A.L. 1947. *Cultural and Natural Areas of Native North
America.* University of California Publications in
American Archeology and Ethnology, vol. 38.

Large, R.G. 1957. *The Skeena: River of Destiny.* Vancouver:
Mitchell Press. Reprint 1966 (6th ed.), Surrey, B.C.:
Heritage House Publishing Co.

Lane, Barbara S. 1951. The Cowichan knitting industry. In
Anthropology in British Columbia, no. 2. Victoria: British
Columbia Provincial Museum.

La Violette, F.E. 1961. *The Struggle for Survival: Indian Cultures
and the Protestant Ethic in British Columbia.* Toronto:
University of Toronto Press.

Lemert, E.M. 1954. *Alcohol and the Northwest Coast Indians.*
Berkley / Los Angeles: University of California Press.

————. 1955. The life and death of an Indian state. *Human Organization* 13:3.

McKelvie, B.A. 1947. *Fort Langley: Outpost of Empire*. Toronto: The Southam Printing Co. Reprint, 1957, Toronto: Thomas Nelson and Sons.

————. 1949. *Tales of Conflict*. Vancouver: *Daily Province*.

McLoughlin, John. 1941. *The Letters of John McLoughlin, First Series, 1825-38*. Edited by E.E. Rich. Toronto: The Champlain Society.

Mills, David. 1877. Letter to Lt-Col I.W. Powell. August 2 1877. Provincial Archives, Victoria.

Moeran, J.W.W. 1923. *McCullagh of Aiyansh*. London: Marshall Brothers.

Mooney, James. 1928. Aboriginal population of America north of Mexico. *Smithsonian Miscellaneous Collections* 80:7.

Morice, A.G. 1895. Notes, archaeological, industrial and sociological, on the Western Denes, with an ethnographical sketch of the same. *Transactions of the Canadian Institute* 4:1-222.

————. 1904. *The History of the Northern Interior of British Columbia (Formerly New Caledonia), 1660-1880*. Toronto: William Briggs.

————. 1910. *History of the Catholic Church in Western Canada, from Lake Superior to the Pacific (1659-1895)*. Toronto: The Musson Book Co.

————. 1923. *Histoire de 1'Eglise Catholique dans 1'Ouest Canadien*. 4 vols. Montreal: n.p.

————. 1932. *The Carrier Language (Dene Family): A Grammar and Dictionary Combined*. 2 vols. Vienna: Verlag der Internationalen Zeitschrift "Anthropos".

Pierce, William H. 1933. *From Potlatch to Pulpit, Being the Autobiography of Rev. William Henry Pierce*, edited by J.P. Hicks. Vancouver: The Vancouver Bindery.

Powell, I.W. 1880 and 1882. Correspondence in the Record Group (RG10), Black Series files of the Department of Indian Affairs at the National Archives of Canada. [Editor's note: The British Columbia Archives

(Information Management Services) has copies of these files. See Young 1992 for more information.]

Ravenhill, Alice. 1944. *A Corner Stone of Canadian Culture: An Outline of the Arts and Crafts of the Indian Tribes of British Columbia.* Occasional Papers, no. 5. Victoria: British Columbia Provincial Museum.

Ray, Verne F. 1939. *Cultural Relations in the Plateau of Northwestern America.* Publication of the Frederick Webb Hodge Anniversary Publications Fund. Los Angeles: Southwest Museum.

Rickard, T.A. 1939. The use of iron and copper by the Indians of British Columbia. *British Columbia Historical Quarterly* 3:25-50.

Shankel, G.E. 1945. The development of Indian policy in British Columbia. Ph.D. thesis, History Dept, University of Washington, Seattle.

Suttles, Wayne P. 1951. The early diffusion of the potato among the Coast Salish. *Southwestern Journal of Anthropology* 7:3.

———. 1954. Post-contact culture change among the Lummi Indians. *British Columbia Historical Quarterly*, vol. 18.

———. 1957. The plateau prophet dance among the Coast Salish. *Southwestern Journal of Anthropology* 13:4.

———. 1963. The persistence of intervillage ties among the Coast Salish. *Ethnology* 2:4.

Taylor, H.C., Jr. 1963. Aboriginal populations of the lower Northwest Coast. *Pacific Northwest Quarterly* 54:4.

Taylor, H.C., Jr, and Wilson Duff. 1956. A post-contact southward movement of the Kwakiutl. *Research Studies* (Washington State University) 24:1.

Thompson, F.W. 1951. Employment problems and economic status of the British Columbia Indians. Master's thesis, University of British Columbia.

Wellcome, H.S. 1887. *The Story of Metlakahtla.* 2nd edition. New York: Saxon.

Wike, Joyce A. 1951. The effect of the maritime fur trade on Northwest Coast Indian society. Ph.D. thesis, Columbia University.

Suggested Reading, 1997

Abbott, Donald N., ed. 1981. *The World Is As Sharp As A Knife: An Anthology in Honour of Wilson Duff*. Victoria: British Columbia Provincial Museum.

Boyd, Robert T. 1990. Demographic history, 1774-1874. In *Handbook of North American Indians*. Vol. 7: *Northwest Coast*, edited by Wayne Suttles. Washington, D.C.: Smithsonian Institution.

British Columbia. 1992. *A Guide to Aboriginal Organizations and Services in British Columbia, 1994-95*. Victoria: Ministry of Aboriginal Affairs.

Cassidy, Frank. 1991. *Reaching Just Settlements: Land Claims in British Columbia*. Lantzville, B.C.: Oolichan Books.

Cole, Douglas, and Ira Chaikin. 1990. *An Iron Hand Upon the People: The Law Against the Potlatch on the Northwest Coast*. Vancouver: Douglas & McIntyre.

Fisher, Robin. 1977. *Contact and Conflict: Indian-European Relations in British Columbia, 1774-1890*. Vancouver: University of British Columbia Press.

Fladmark, Knut R. 1986. *British Columbia Prehistory*. Ottawa: National Museums of Canada.

Harris, Cole. 1994. Voices of disaster: smallpox around the Strait of Georgia in 1792. Ethnohistory 41:4:591-626.

Helm, June, ed. 1981. *Handbook of North American Indians*. Vol. 6: *Subarctic*. Washington, D.C.: Smithsonian Institution.

Jensen, Doreen, and Cheryl Brooks, eds. 1991. *In Celebration of
    Our Survival: The First Nations of British Columbia. B.C.
    Studies*, no. 89, University of British Columbia.
Kirk, Ruth. 1986. *Wisdom of the Elders: Native Traditions on the
    Northwest Coast*. Vancouver: Douglas & McIntyre.
Kennedy, Dorothy I.D. 1994. *A Reference Guide to the
    Establishment of Indian Reserves in British Columbia
    1849-1911*. Victoria: British Columbia Indian Language
    Project. (Prepared for: Claims Research and
    Assessment Directorate, Indian and Northern Affairs,
    Ottawa.)
McMillan, Alan D. 1988. *Native Peoples and Cultures of Canada:
    An Anthropological Overview*. Vancouver: Douglas &
    McIntyre.
Mills, Antonia. 1994. *Eagle Down is Our Law: Witsuwit'en Law,
    Feasts and Land Claims*. Vancouver: University of
    British Columbia Press.
Perrault, Jeanne, and Sylvia Vance, eds. 1990. *Writing the Circle:
    Native Women of Western Canada*. Edmonton: NeWest
    Publishers.
Suttles, Wayne, ed. 1990. *Handbook of North American Indians*.
    Vol. 7: *Northwest Coast*. Washington, D.C.: Smithsonian
    Institution.
Tennant, Paul. 1990. *Aboriginal Peoples and Politics: The Indian
    Land Question in British Columbia, 1849-1989*.
    Vancouver: University of British Columbia Press.
Wa,Gisday and Delgam Uukw. 1989. *The Spirit in the Land*. (The
    opening statement of the Gitksan and Wet'suwet'en
    Hereditary Chiefs in the Supreme Court of British
    Columbia, 11 May 1987.) Gabriola, B.C.: Reflections.
Webster, Peter S. 1983. *As Far As I Know: Reminiscences of an
    Ahousat Elder*. Campbell River, B.C.: Campbell River
    Museum and Archives.
Young, Terry Ann. 1992. *Researching the History of Aboriginal
    Peoples in British Columbia: A Guide to Resources at the
    British Columbia Archives and Records Service and B.C.
    Lands*. Victoria: B.C. Lands.

Index

absolute title – 85, 86, 92n
Adams, Alfred – 155
agencies/agents, Indian – *See* Indian agencies.
Aiyansh – 30, 140, 151
Alaska – 74, 98, 110, 116, 125n, 136, 139, 155, 156
alcohol/liquor – 16, 54, 61, 67, 72, 77, 79, 101, 137
Alert Bay – 70, 71, 81, 90, 103, 123, 129, 140, 141, 152
alliances, First Nations:
  Allied Tribes of British Columbia – 96, 97, 155;
  Native Brotherhood of British Columbia – 127, 155-56, 157
  other native brotherhoods – 97, 108, 155, 156, 157
  Pacific Coast Native Fishermen's Assoc. – 156
Anglican Church – *See* churches.
argillite – 82, 113, 115, 118-19, 120
assimilation – 64, 66, 87, 88, 106, 107
Astoria, Fort – *See* Fort.

Athapaskan – 20, 22, 25, 47-51, 55, 80, 117, 134, 135, 165
Babine (people) – 26, 48, 70, 90
band
  councils – 102, 155
  system – 51, 154
Barbeau, Marius – 74, 110, 112, 163
Beaver (people) – 22, 51, 83, 91, 98, 99, 165
Bella Bella
  (people) – 30, 59, 62
  (village) – 30, 70, 77, 90, 142, 143
Bella Coola
  (people) – 10, 20, 21, 22, 35, 55, 90, 110, 124, 165
  (village) – 35, 60, 90, 142, 143
  River – 56, 76
Beynon, William – 155
Bini – 131
Boas, Franz – 110
Calder, Frank – 105
Canyon City – 29, 145, 156
Carrier – 22, 25, 80, 90, 131, 132, 134, 135, 165

Catholic Church / Catholics – *See* churches.

ceremonial life – 26, 72, 79, 88, 152

ceremonies, aboriginal – 80, 82, 124, 130, 147, 148. *See also* winter ceremonies.

Chilcotin – 22, 90, 115, 134, 135, 165

Church Missionary Society – 129, 136

churches:

Anglican – 88, 128, 129, 135, 136-41, 141, 142, 144

Catholic – 88, 128, 129, 131, 132-35, 140, 141, 150

Congregational – 143

Methodist – 129, 140, 141-43, 144

Pentecostal – 88, 129, 145

Presbyterian – 143

Salvation Army – 88, 128, 129, 143-45, 157

Shaker – 88, 129, 132, 145-46

United Church – 88, 128, 143. *See also* missionaries.

Coast Salish – *See* Salish.

Coast Tsimshian – *See* Tsimshian.

collections/collectors – 109-112, 119, 127

Collison, Rev. W.H. – 111, 140, 151

Columbia River – 54, 76, 77, 79, 131

Comox (people) – 22, 36, 83, 90, 165

Cook, Captain James – 74, 75, 77, 108, 109

copper – 75, 78

Cowichan – 26, 38, 70, 86, 115, 116, 127, 133

Cranmer, Doug – 123, 124, 125

Cree – 51, 90, 99

crests – 74, 149, 150, 152

Crosby, Rev. Thomas – 141, 142, 143

Dakelh – 165. *See also* Carrier.

Dawson, G.M. – 109

Demers, Rev. Modeste – 132, 133

diseases – 54, 58, 59, 60, 67, 76

introduced – 16, 54, 58, 72

epidemics – 26-27, 54, 58-60, 137

smallpox – 44, 54, 58-59, 60, 76, 137

tuberculosis – 60, 67

Doolan, Rev. R.A. – 140, 142

Douglas, James – 58, 84, 85, 86, 93, 132, 136-37

Duncan, William – 60, 129, 136-39, 142, 150

Dunne-za – 165. *See also* Beaver.

economy,

aboriginal – 16, 67, 73, 79, 104, 106, 107, 126-28

non-aboriginal – 86, 106, 127

Edenshaw, Chief Albert Edward – 118, 151

education – 67, 97, 100, 102-4, 105, 128, 157

employment – 66, 88

firearms – *See* guns.

food – 56, 77, 126-27

Fort

Astoria – 76

Babine – 49

Connolly – 133

Durham – 77

George – 47

Langley – 13, 77, 129, 132

McLeod – 73, 133

McLoughlin – 77

Nelson – 51, 99

Rupert – 26, 32, 59, 60, 77, 80, 85, 133, 140

Simpson – 58-59, 77, 80, 136

St George – 133

St James – 48, 134
St John – 90, 98, 99
Vancouver – 54, 76, 129, 132
Victoria – 41, 77, 129, 132
Ware – 49
Fraser, Simon – 76, 77
Fraser
  River – 56, 76, 86, 89, 133, 141
  Valley – 117, 128, 129, 130, 133,
    141, 143
Gedanst – 143
Ghost Dance of the Plains – 132
Gitksan – 19, 22, 25, 29, 90, 123, 125,
  165
Gladstone, Charles – 120
gold rush – 59
Great Settlement of 1927 – 97
Green, Jonathon S. – 58, 135-36
Greenville – 139, 142, 145, 156
guns/firearms – 54, 61, 75, 76,
  78, 79, 83
Hagwilget – 133
Haida – 20, 22, 25, 26, 27, 55, 58,
  59, 62, 78, 80, 82, 90, 98, 116,
  118-19, 119, 120, 123, 123-24,
  124, 125, 130, 136, 140, 143, 165
Haisla – 22, 30, 90, 165
Halkomelem – 22, 37-40, 165
Hazelton – 29, 90, 117, 140, 143,
  144, 152
Heiltsuk – 22, 26, 62, 165
Hesquiat Mission – 133
horse – 76, 79, 83, 131
Hudson's Bay Company – 27, 73,
  75, 76, 77, 80, 84, 85, 92, 98
Hudson Hope – 51, 99
Hunt, Henry – 123, 124
income, aboriginal – 67, 101, 114,
  115, 127
Indian Act – 64, 100, 101, 150, 155
Indian Advisory Committee – 105
Indian Affairs
  Branch – 10, 17, 25, 64, 65,
    66n, 87, 89, 100, 101, 102,
    104, 105, 115, 155
  Joint Committee – 98
  Royal Commission – 94, 100n
Indian agencies – 64, 65, 66n, 69n,
  89, 90, 91, 98, 99, 100, 101, 155
  agents – 18, 61, 89, 95, 150
  Commissioner – 88, 101, 110,
    138
  Superintendent – 101, 102, 154
Indian and Northern Health
  Services – 102, 104
Indian Claims Commission – 98,
  157
Indian Department – 61-62, 100
Indian title – 86, 87, 91-98, 98. See
  also Land Question.
Indian Trust Fund – 102
Inland Tlingit – 20, 22, 52, 80, 90.
  See also Tlingit.
integration – 70, 106, 107
intermarriage – 16, 25, 66, 80. See
  also marriage.
iron / iron tools – 75, 77, 78, 82,
  108
jade – 115, 120
Jefferies, William – 124
jewellery – 109, 115, 118, 120
Kamloops – 45, 89, 90, 134, 135,
  153
Kaska – 22, 51, 90, 99, 165
Kelly, Peter – 96, 97
Kincolith – 29, 52, 90, 140, 142,
  145, 156
kinship – 15, 21, 24-25, 108, 149,
  150, 152, 153, 154
Kispiox – 19, 29, 140, 143, 144
Kitkatla – 28, 54, 140
Kitsegukla – 29, 141, 143, 145, 152
Kitselas – 29, 123, 145
Kitwancool – 10, 29, 125, 140-41,
  142
Kitwanga – 29, 123, 140-41

Kootenay – 10, 20, 22, 24, 26, 46,
    55, 83, 90, 132, 135, 165
Ktunaxa – 10, 165. *See also*
    Kootenay.
Kwakiutl – 9-10, 17, 20, 20-21, 22,
    25, 30-33, 55, 62, 78, 80, 81, 82,
    83, 88, 90, 111, 121, 122, 123,
    124, 125, 127, 129, 133, 140,
    141, 143, 147, 150, 165
    Northern Kwakiutl – 25, 26,
        30, 62, 156
    Southern Kwakiutl – 22, 26,
        30-33, 83, 90, 123, 156
Kwakwaka'wakw – 10, 111, 165.
    See also Kwakiutl.
Lakes (people) – 22, 46
Land Question – 86n, 87, 89, 93,
    95, 98, 155, 156. *See also* Indian
    title.
Langley, Fort – *See* Fort.
Lejacq, Father Jean – 132, 134
Lillooet
    (people) – 22, 25, 43, 90, 114,
        115, 135, 165
    (settlement) – 43, 60, 120
liquor – *See* alcohol.
logging – 15, 127-28, 128
Lytton
    (band) – 42, 70, 141
    (settlement) – 41, 42, 90, 117,
        120, 128, 135, 141
marriage – 64, 65, 66, 130, 150,
    154. *See also* intermarriage.
Martin, Mungo – 120, 122, 124,
    125, 153
masks – 82, 109, 120, 122, 147, 149,
    150
Masset – 27, 59, 70, 90, 116, 140,
    151, 155
McKenna, J.A.J. – 94
Methodist Church – *See* churches.
Metlakatla – 28, 60, 129, 136-39,
    140, 142, 144, 150

New Metlakatla – 136, 139
missionaries – 18, 58, 72, 73, 88,
    95, 107, 110, 128-29, 129, 131,
    132-45, 149, 150, 151, 154. *See
    also* churches.
model poles – 119, 121, 122
Morice, A.G. – 133, 134
Mudge, Cape – 33, 60, 83, 143, 156
museums – 108, 109, 110-12,
    116n, 119, 122
    American Museum of Natural
        History – 110, 119
    (British Columbia) Provincial
        Museum – 9, 110, 111, 112,
        122, 124, 125
    Royal British Columbia
        Museum – 8, 68n, 124n.
Nanaimo
    (people) – 24, 37
    (settlement) – 37, 60, 85, 129,
        141, 143, 147, 151
Nass
    (people) – 29, 95, 96
    River – 50, 52, 56, 77, 95, 124,
        139, 142, 145, 152, 156
native brotherhoods – *See*
    alliances.
Native Voice, The – 156
New Caledonia – 76, 129, 132
Newcombe, C.F. – 12, 110, 111,
    112
New Metlakatla – *See* Metlakatla.
New Westminster – 64, 69, 89,
    90, 133, 134
Nicola (people) – 22, 23, 42, 45, 52
Nisga'a – 10, 165. *See also* Niska.
Nishga
    (people) – *See* Niska
    Land Committee – 96, 155, 156
    Petition – 96, 156
    Tribal Council – 97, 156, 157
Niska – 10, 22, 25, 29-30, 52, 90,
    123, 165

Nlaka'pamux – 165. *See also*
    Thompson.
Nootka
    (people) – 9, 20, 20-21, 22, 25,
        33-35, 55, 62, 78, 80, 83, 90,
        108, 115, 124, 128, 129, 133,
        135, 143, 156, 157, 165
    (place) – 74, 76, 132
North Vancouver – 37, 70, 147,
    153
North West Company – 73, 76
Nuu-chah-nulth – 9, 165. *See also*
    Nootka (people).
Nuxalk – 10, 165. *See also* Bella
    Coola.
Okanagan – 22, 45-46, 52, 70, 90,
    132, 135, 165
Oweekeno – 165. *See also*
    Kwakiutl.
Paull, Andrew – 96, 97, 156
Peace River – 51, 76, 83, 99
Pentecostal Church – *See*
    churches.
Pentlatch – 22, 23, 36-37
political organization – 21, 23,
    24, 25, 88, 107, 108, 134, 149,
    154-57. *See also* alliances.
Port
    Essington – 28, 29, 142, 144
    Simpson – 26, 28, 58, 60, 70,
        104n, 136-37, 141, 143, 144,
        145, 155, 156
potlatch – 26, 79, 80, 81-82, 101,
    109, 126, 135, 137, 148, 149-50,
    153
Powell, Dr I.W. – 88, 89, 110, 138,
    139
Privy Council – 96, 97
prophets / prophet cults – 128,
    129-32, 132, 145
Puget Sound – 83, 132, 145, 147
Quadra, Commandant Juan
    Francisco Bodega y – 74, 76

Queen Charlotte Islands – 56, 59,
    74, 90, 118, 140, 143
registered Indians – 63, 64-66, 67,
    155
Reid, Bill – 120, 124, 125
Reserve Commission – 26, 94, 95,
    96-97, 100
reserve land – 93, 95, 97, 100,
    101, 102
reserves, First Nations – 26, 64,
    65, 66, 68, 69, 70, 71, 85, 86, 87,
    91-98, 100, 101, 102, 104, 148
residential schools – *See* schools.
Revolving Loan Fund – 101, 102
Ridley, Bishop William – 136, 139
rituals – 88, 128, 130, 131-32, 135,
    137, 139, 144, 145, 147, 148, 149
Royal Commission on Indian
    Affairs – *See* Reserve
    Commission.
Russians – 74, 76, 119, 132
Salish,
    Coast – 20, 21, 22, 24, 36-41, 55,
        62, 83, 90, 113, 117, 124, 130,
        131, 134, 135, 141, 143, 147,
        149, 152, 152-53, 156, 157
    Interior – 20, 22, 24, 25, 41-46,
        55, 90, 96, 115, 117, 130, 147,
        156
Salteaux – *See* Cree.
Salvation Army – *See* churches.
schools – 70, 99, 102-3, 133, 137,
    139, 141, 142, 144
    residential schools – 102-3,
        120, 135, 141, 143
Sea Otter – 75, 79, 118
Sechelt
    (people) – 22, 36, 115, 134, 165
    (settlement) – 36, 134, 135
Secwepemc – 10, 165. *See also*
    Shuswap.
Sekani – 22, 24, 49-50, 83, 90, 99,
    100, 165

settlement patterns – 68, 71, 86, 98

settlements,
  aboriginal – 27-52, 68, 69-70
  colonial – 13, 16, 73, 74, 76, 86, 91, 98, 106, 126, 132

Shaker Church – See churches.

shamanism/shamans – 108, 109, 135, 137, 147

Shuswap – 10, 22, 43-45, 46, 90, 132, 135, 165

silverwork – 113, 115, 119-20

Skedans – 26, 27, 124

Skeena River – 26, 56, 80, 90, 123, 127, 129, 130, 140, 143, 145, 152

Skidegate – 22, 27, 119, 143, 151

Slave (people) – 22, 49, 51, 90, 98, 99-100, 165

slavery – 149, 150

Slocum, John – 145

smallpox – See diseases.

Smith, Harlan I. – 110, 123

Smohalla cult – 131

social
  customs – 106, 149, 150, 152
  development – 16, 104n
  life – 72, 88, 108, 109, 153, 157
  organization – 23, 24, 79, 80, 149-53, 154
  structures – 71, 107, 126, 134, 135, 138, 149, 151, 152

Spain / the Spanish – 74, 75, 76, 92n, 111, 132

spirit dance – 108, 147-49, 152-53, 153

Squamish (people) – 22, 37, 70, 96, 115, 141, 165

St Mary's Mission – See missionaries.

St Michael's Mission – See missionaries.

Stikine River – 50, 80, 140

Tahltan – 22, 25, 65n, 69n, 80, 90, 128, 140, 141, 165

Tanoo – 26, 25, 27, 143

technology – 106, 127
  aboriginal – 72, 87-88, 107-8, 108, 116
  non-aboriginal – 106, 108

Telegraph Creek – 100, 135, 140

Thompson (people) – 22, 26, 41-42, 52, 90, 115, 129, 135, 165

Thompson, David – 76

Tlingit – 22, 52, 54, 80, 98, 109, 116, 119, 136, 165. See also Inland Tlingit.

Tomlinson, Rev. R. – 140

totem poles – 74, 77, 81, 82, 109, 112, 115, 120, 121, 122-25, 150
  model – See model poles.

trading posts – 61, 76, 80, 106, 139. See also Fort.

Transformer Haylse – 77

trapping – 14, 127, 128

treaties – 85, 86, 91, 92, 93, 96, 97, 98, 99, 101, 102

Treaty No. 8 – 92, 98-100

Tsetsaut – 18, 22, 23, 52

Tsilhqot'in – 165. See also Chilcotin.

Tsimshian – 20, 22, 25, 26, 28-30, 55, 58, 62, 80, 90, 123, 136, 137, 138, 140, 141, 142, 143, 155-56, 165
  Coast Tsimshian – 26, 155, 157

United Church – See churches.

Vancouver – 90, 112, 119, 122, 123, 143, 144, 145, 156

Vancouver, Captain George – 76, 83, 109

Vancouver, North – See North Vancouver.

Vancouver Island – 56, 60, 83, 84, 85, 86, 89, 90, 92, 98, 116, 117, 129, 133, 143, 147, 148, 157

Victoria – 58, 85, 89, 94, 110, 112,
114, 117, 119, 123, 124, 129,
133, 136-37, 137, 139, 141, 142,
143, 144, 145, 146, 147, 148
Victoria, Fort – *See* Fort.
villages,
Christian – 60, 129, 135, 137-
39, 140, 142, 144, 145
First Nations – 20, 25, 27-52,
56, 59, 61, 68, 70, 82, 83,
108, 112-13, 123, 125, 129,
136, 140, 141, 142, 143, 145,
148, 152, 155, 156

village sites – 15, 24, 86
Vowell, A.W. – 89, 94
wars – 16, 53, 58, 61, 80, 82, 83,
93, 150
welfare – 100, 104-5, 105, 114, 156
Williams Lake – 43, 60, 90, 134,
135, 153
winter ceremonies / winter
dance – 101, 109, 147, 149-50,
150

The Indian History of British Columbia
   The Impact of the White Man

Wilson Duff

Printing history:
   First edition   1964
   Second edition   1969
      Reprinted   1973, 1977, 1980, 1985, 1987, 1992
   Third edition   1997
      Reprinted   2004, 2010, 2014
      Print-on-demand 2022

Third edition, 1997:
Edited, designed and typeset by Gerry Truscott. (Typeset in
   Palatino 11/14, with titles and captions in Poppl-Laudatio.)
Editorial consultation by Grant Keddie and Alan Hoover.
Photographic consultation by Dan Savard.
Manuscript preparation by Sally Sproule.
Proof reading by Tara Steigenberger.

Reprint, 2014:
Cover design by Stuart Wootton, form-creative.ca.